Grammar for Conversation • 영어가 술술 나오는 왕초보 회화 문법

Grammar
Chat

PAGODA Books

Grammar
Chat

초판　1쇄　인쇄　2008년　3월 22일
개정판 3쇄 발행　2023년　9월 18일

지 은 이 | 파고다교육그룹 언어교육연구소
펴 낸 이 | 박경실
펴 낸 곳 | **PAGODA Books** 파고다북스
출판등록 | 2005년 5월 27일 제 300-2005-90호
주　　소 | 06614 서울특별시 서초구 강남대로 419, 19층(서초동, 파고다타워)
전　　화 | (02) 6940-4070
팩　　스 | (02) 536-0660
홈페이지 | www.pagodabook.com

ISBN 978-89-6281-826-0 (13740)

파고다북스	www.pagodabook.com
파고다 어학원	www.pagoda21.com
파고다 인강	www.pagodastar.com
테스트 클리닉	www.testclinic.com

| 낙장 및 파본은 구매처에서 교환해 드립니다.

Grammar for Conversation • 영어가 술술 나오는 왕초보 회화 문법

Grammar
Chat

About This Book

이 책의 내용에 관하여

<Grammar Chat>은 영어 회화 실력을 향상시켜 주는 초급자 수준의 회화 문법 교재입니다. 기존의 문법 자체만을 강조하는 문법책과는 달리, 이 책은 각 Unit에 있는 문법 사항을 활용하여 실생활의 말하기와 듣기에 적용하는 데에 주안점을 두었습니다. <Grammar Chat>은 학생들이 문법적 지식을 이용해 실제 생활 회화에 접목할 수 있도록 해줄 것입니다.

Grammar Chat은 :

▶ 기초 회화를 위한 전체 문법을 아우르는 20개의 Unit으로 구성되었습니다.

▶ 각 Unit의 문법 요소는 몇 가지 세부 문법 항목으로 구성이 되어 있으며, 이를 통해 자세한 문법을 공부하고 회화와 접목하여 학습할 수 있습니다.

▶ 생생한 외국인 회화 발음을 들을 수 있는 무료 MP3 파일이 포함되어 있습니다.

▶ 휴대하면서 단어를 외울 수 있도록 단어장 PDF 파일을 다운로드 받을 수 있습니다.

▶ Let's Speak!의 샘플 정답을 다운로드하여 학습할 수 있습니다.

* MP3 파일, 단어장 PDF 파일, 단어장 음성 파일, Let's Speak! 샘플 정답 다운로드 :

www.pagodabook.com

▶ 교재 및 학습법
소개 동영상 보기

각 unit의 구성 및 특징

Get Started

대화, 이메일, 조리법 등 다양한 형식으로 각 Part 에서 설명할 문법 사항에 관한 전반적인 소개를 하는 부분입니다. 학습할 문법 사항은 파란색 글씨로 표시되어 있습니다.

Focus

각 Part에서 다루는 문법 사항에 관한 본격적인 설명 단계입니다. 한국어로 알기 쉬운 설명이 되어 있으며, 이해를 돕기 위해 다양한 표와 삽화가 등장합니다.

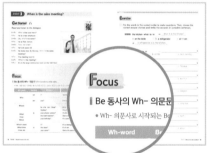

Exercise

Focus 부분에서 학습한 내용을 연습할 수 있도록 방대한 문제들이 수록되어 있습니다. 많은 문제를 풀면서 문법 패턴을 확실히 익힐 수 있습니다.

Let's Speak!

학습한 문법 사항을 이용하여 파트너, 혹은 그룹 activities를 통해 실제 생활에서 일어나는 대화를 연습할 수 있도록 해줍니다. 듣기와 말하기 연습을 할 수 있으며, 이전 Unit에서 배운 문법 사항까지도 활용하여 활용할 수 있도록 해줍니다. 샘플 정답을 다운로드하여 학습할 수 있습니다.

Contents

About This Book 이 책의 내용에 관하여

Contents 목차

Contents

★ MP3 파일, 단어장 PDF 파일, 단어장 음성파일, Let's Speak! 샘플 정답 다운로드 : www.pagodabook.com

UNIT 01

Simple Present of *Be* verb

Be동사의 현재시제

PART 1 I am a sales assistant.

Get Started 🎧

1-1. mp3

Read and listen to the passage.

My name is Julia. I am a sales assistant at Blue Ocean.
It's a big shopping mall downtown. My working hours
are very long, but the pay isn't that good.

My manager is Pamela. She is very kind and generous.
My coworkers are very friendly. Some customers
aren't very nice. But I am happy with my job.

Focus

| Be 동사 (Be verb) **: am / is / are**

- Be 동사 다음에는 명사, 형용사, 또는 전치사 구(전치사 + 명사)가 따라 나옵니다.

  Be + 명사: Tom is a teacher. | Be + 형용사: Tom is smart. | Be + 전치사 구: Tom is in the living room.

- 주어의 인칭(I, you, he / she, they)에 따라 달라지는 Be동사의 형태에 유의하세요.

1. Be 동사의 긍정문 (Affirmative Statements)

Singular			Plural		
Subject	**Be Verb**		**Subject**	**Be Verb**	
I	**am**	an accountant.	We / Tom and I	**are**	accountants.
You	**are**	kind.	You / You and Tom	**are**	kind.
He / She Tom / Tina	**is**	happy. a student.	They / Tom and Tina	**are**	happy. students.
It The book	**is**	on the desk.	They / The books	**are**	on the desk.

> **긍정문에서의 축약형**(Contracted Form): 구어체에서는 다음과 같이 be동사의 모음을 부분적으로 삭제하고, 어포스트로피(')를 붙여 축약된 형태를 사용하는 경향이 있습니다.

I am = **I'm**

He is / She is / It is = **He's / She's / It's**

You are / We are / They are = **You're / We're / They're**

2 Be 동사의 부정문 (Negative Statements)

Singular		Plural	
I **am not**	an accountant.	We **are not**	accountants.
You **are not**	kind.	You **are not**	kind.
He / She **is not**	happy. a student.	They **are not**	happy. students. on the desk.
It **is not**	on the desk.		

> **부정문에서의 축약형**(Contracted Form): 주어가 He / She / It / You / We / They일 경우, 주어와 be동사를 축약하는 방법과 be동사와 not을 축약하는 방법 두 가지를 사용할 수 있습니다.

He is not / She is not / It is not = **He's not / She's not / It's not**

                                  = **He isn't / She isn't / It isn't**

You are not / We are not / They are not = **You're not / We're not / They're not**

                                                = **You aren't / We aren't / They aren't**

I am not의 경우, **I'm not**으로만 축약이 가능합니다.

Exercise

(A) Fill in the blanks with the correct simple present forms of *be* verbs.

> **Example**   Kevin ___is___ from Venezuela.

1. I _____ a professor.

2. Tom and Susan _____ siblings.

3. It _____ 10:30 in the morning.

4. You _____ always late.

5. She _____ kind to everyone.

6. My name _____ Danni.

7. Gwen and I _____ 25 years old.

8. Canberra _____ the capital of Australia.

B Rewrite the sentences using contracted forms.

Example   The professor is not happy with the report.

➡   The professor isn't happy with the report.

1. I am not in bed.

➡ _____

2. Both movies are not popular.

➡ _____

3. The capital of Australia is not Sydney.

➡ _____

4. You and I are not from Italy.

➡ _____

5. My cats are not on the couch.

➡ _____

6. Grant is not a voice actor.

➡ _____

7. They are not in line.

➡ _____

8. It is not cold outside.

➡ _____

C Put the words in the correct order to make complete sentences.

Example at / students / not / some / math / good / are

➡ Some students are not good at math.

1. are / Canada / from / we ➡ _____

2. am / not / I / a student ➡ _____

3. big / the classrooms / aren't ➡ _____

4. not / is / a ball / it ➡ _____

5. love / in / not / they / are ➡ _____

6. best friends / are / Freddy / Fiona / and ➡ _____

7. and / Julia / are / a couple / David ➡ _____

8. is / diligent / Jack / not ➡ _____

D Complete the dialogues by using the correct affirmative and negative simple present forms of *be* verbs.

1. Mark: How _____ you today, Melissa?
   Melissa: I _____ fine. How about you?
   Mark: I _____ so worried. The final exams _____ next week.
   Melissa: That's true. But I _____ worried.
   Mark: Why not?
   Melissa: Because I _____ in a study group now.

2. Kristin: Hi, my name _____ Kristin. I _____ a new student.
   Scott: Nice to meet you, Kristin. I _____ Scott.
   Kristin: Scott, what's your major?
   Scott: My major _____ Biology.
   Kristin: Wow, same here. How are the classes?
   Scott: All the classes _____ great, except Professor Smith's class.
   Kristin: Why is that?
   Scott: Because his lecture _____ so boring.

E Change the affirmative statements into negative statements.

> **Example** They are very famous actors.
>
> → _____They are not very famous actors._____

1. My dog is very cute.

   → _____

2. We're good at speaking English.

   → _____

3. My older sister is a nurse.

   → _____

4. All the office workers are from different countries.

   → _____

5. My mom and dad are in the Philippines.

   → _____

6. Bottles of water are in the refrigerator.

   → _____

7. That song is popular all over the world.

   → _____

8. I'm in charge of hiring new employees.

   → _____

PART 2

Are they in the meeting room?

Get Started

1-2. mp3

Read and listen to the dialogue.

James: Jane, you look pale. **Are you** OK?
Jane: **No, I'm not.** I'm so nervous.
James: **Are you** worried about the presentation?
Jane: Yes, I am. **Are the clients** in the meeting room now?
James: Yes, they are.
Jane: OK. Let me get my documents.
James: **Are you** ready?
Jane: No, not really. But I'll give it a try.

Focus

▌Be 동사의 Yes / No 의문문과 짧은 응답 (Yes / No Questions and Short Answers)

● [Be 동사 + 주어 + 명사 / 형용사 / 전치사 구]의 형태로 만들어집니다.

Yes / No Questions			Short Answers	
Be Verb	**Subject**		**Affirmative**	**Negative**
Am	I	late?	Yes, you are.	No, you are not.
Are	you	a student?	Yes, I am.	No, I am not.
Is	he / she / it	in the office?	Yes, he / she / it is.	No, he / she / it is not.
Are	we / you / they	ready?	Yes, you / we / they are.	No, you / we / they are not.

> ❭ 의문문에 대한 긍정의 답변에서는 축약형을 사용하지 않고, 부정의 답변에서만 축약형을 사용할 수 있습니다.
>
> Yes, he's. (✗) | Yes, I'm. (✗) | No, I'm not. (◯) | No, he isn't. (◯)

Exercise

(A) Match the questions with the correct answers.

1. Is he an engineer? •   • a. Yes, they are.

2. Is Thailand hot these days? •   • b. No, it is not. It's very old.

3. Are you happy? •   • c. Yes, it is.

4. Are they good at Spanish? •   • d. No, he isn't. He is a police officer.

5. Is this computer new? •   • e. No, you aren't. You are on time.

6. Are you all thirsty? •   • f. Yes, I am so happy.

7. Am I late for this class? •   • g. Yes, we are.

(B) Use the words given and the correct forms of *be* verbs to make questions. Then, complete the short answers. When you answer 'No', add your own words.

> **Example**   your car / big
>
> → Q: ____Is your car big?____   A: ____No, it isn't. It's small.____

1. the textbooks / expensive

    → Q: _____

    A: Yes, _____

2. I / on time

    → Q: _____

    A: No, _____

3. this book / yours

    → Q: _____

    A: No, _____

4. German / your native language

    → Q: _____

    A: Yes, _____

5. your best friend / from Korea?

→ Q: _____ _____

A: Yes, _____

6. you and I / on the same team

→ Q: _____

A: No, _____

Ⓒ **Complete the dialogues by using the correct simple present forms of *be* verbs.**

1. A: _____ they new sunglasses?

B: Yes, they are. I got them in a duty-free store.

A: They _____ very nice and fancy.

B: Thanks. _____ your coat made of real fur?

A: Hmm... no, it _____. It _____ an imitation.

B: Oh, really? It looks like real fur.

2. A: _____ the capital of Korea Busan?

B: No, it _____. The capital of Korea _____ Seoul.

A: Let's see... How about Italy? _____ the capital of Italy Rome?

B: Yes, it _____. People sometimes think it _____ Milano, but it

_____.

3. A: _____ you new here?

B: Yes, I _____.

A: Oh, welcome to Sunnydale dormitory.

B: Thanks. _____ you happy here?

A: Yes, I _____. Everybody here _____ very friendly and nice.

B: That _____ nice. _____ the campus buildings near here?

A: Yes, they _____.

B: How about the gym? _____ it nearby?

A: Of course. It _____ right across the street.

When is the sales meeting?

Get Started

1-3. mp3

Read and listen to the dialogue.

Emily: **Who is** that over there?

Mike: He is a new employee.

Emily: Oh, **what's** his name?

Mike: He is Rick Vernon.

Emily: **How old is** he?

Mike: He's 29 years old.

Emily: He looks nice. By the way, **when is** the sales meeting?

Mike: The meeting is at 10.

Emily: **Where is** the meeting?

Mike: It's in the large conference room on the 19th floor.

Focus

▌ Be 동사의 Wh- 의문문 (Wh-Questions of Be verb)

● Wh- 의문사로 시작되는 Be 동사의 의문문은 [Wh- 의문사 + Be 동사 + 주어…?]의 형태로 만들어집니다.

Wh-word	Be Verb	Subject	Answers
Who	am	I?	You're the captain of this ship.
	are	you?	I'm the manager of this shop.
Where	is	he / she / Jon / Cindy?	He's / She's downstairs.
		Sydney?	It's on the east side of Australia.
What		your phone number?	It's 80-555-3367.
How		the math teacher?	She's nice and clever.
When		your birthday?	It's June 6th.
Which class	is	it?	It's a biology class.
What time		the class?	It's 9 am.
How old		your sister?	She's 30 years old.

Exercise

A Put the words in the correct order to make questions. Then, choose the correct answer choices and write the answers in complete sentences.

Example the kitchen / what / is / in ➡ _What is in the kitchen?_

    a. on the table   (b. a refrigerator)   c. at 11 am

➡ _A refrigerator is in the kitchen._

1. the / kitchen / who's / in ➡ _____ ?
   a. Mr. Kim   b. a little   c. He's cooking.

   ➡ _____

2. over / is / when / class / your ➡ _____ ?
   a. at the market   b. soon   c. Physics

   ➡ _____

3. is / the wedding / where ➡ _____ ?
   a. at the church   b. at 10   c. the fifth

   ➡ _____

4. from / where / you / are ➡ _____ ?
   a. on Sunday   b. from 9 to 6   c. Belgium

   ➡ _____

5. your / job / new / how / is ➡ _____ ?
   a. great   b. near my office   c. very new

   ➡ _____

6. time / is / what / it ➡ _____ ?
   a. Friday   b. 3 o'clock   c. April

   ➡ _____

7. bag / color / is / what / your ➡ _____ ?
   a. beautiful   b. big   c. silver

   ➡ _____

B Find the errors and correct them.

Example **Q**: Who're this woman?   **A**: She am my aunt.
                    is / 's   is / 's

1. **Q**: What are the name of the new guy?   **A**: His name're Kevin.

2. **Q**: Who is Christmas?   **A**: It am on December 25th.

3. **Q**: How are the weather?   **A**: It are cold and windy.

4. **Q**: When're the Labor Day in the U.S.?   **A**: They're in September.

5. **Q**: How much is these earrings?   **A**: It's $10.

6. **Q**: What time are the flight?   **A**: It are 8 pm.

7. **Q**: How are the movie?   **A**: It're OK.

C Complete the dialogues by using the correct wh-words and simple present forms of *be* verbs.

1. **Tom**:   Sorry. _____ I late for this party?

    Amber: Don't worry. You _____ on time.

    Tom: Oh, good.

    Amber: Come on in.

    Tom: Amber, _____ is the person over there?

    Amber: She _____ my neighbor, Hanna.

    Tom: _____ old _____ she?

    Amber: She' ____ 24. _____ you interested in her?

    Tom: Yes, I _____.

2. **Jeff**:   Hello? _____ is this?

    Fiona: This _____ Fiona. _____ Jeff there?

Jeff: Speaking.

Fiona: Hi, Jeff. _____ are you today?

Jeff: I _____ fine. So, _____ 's up?

Fiona: I want to ask you about your English class. _____ the class easy?

Jeff: No, _____. I think it's really hard for beginners.

Fiona: Oh, I see. _____ is the teacher?

Jeff: The teacher _____ Rick Newton.

Fiona: Where _____ he from?

Jeff: He _____ from England.

Fiona: Oh, I see.

3. Ian: _____ _____ your name?

Carol: My name _____ Carol. Nice to meet you.

Ian: Nice to meet you, too. I _____ Ian. Do you live near here?

Carol: Yes. By the way, _____ time _____ _____ now?

Ian: Oh, it _____ 7:40. I hope the bus comes soon.

Carol: I hope so, too. _____ far _____ it to downtown?

Ian: It' ____ only three stops away.

4. Nicole: Wow! What a lovely picture! _____ they your family?

Mr. Kim: Yes, _____ _____.

Nicole: _____ is she next to you?

Mr. Kim: _____ my wife, Helen. She _____ lovely.

Nicole: And _____ they your children?

Mr. Kim: Yes, _____ _____.

Nicole: _____ old _____ they?

Mr. Kim: Philip _____ seven and Sue _____ four years old.

Nicole: They _____ so cute.

Let's Speak!

Activity-1

A Listen to the recordings and check (✓) the correct boxes. 🎧

Questions	Robert	Danni	Ken
1. Is she / he from America?	Yes ☐ No ☐	Yes ☐ No ☐	Yes ☐ No ☐
2. Is she / he married?	Yes ☐ No ☐	Yes ☐ No ☐	Yes ☐ No ☐
3. Is she / he happy with her / his job?	Yes ☐ No ☐	Yes ☐ No ☐	Yes ☐ No ☐
4. Is she / he good at speaking Korean?	Yes ☐ No ☐	Yes ☐ No ☐	Yes ☐ No ☐
5. Is she / he in Korea now?	Yes ☐ No ☐	Yes ☐ No ☐	Yes ☐ No ☐

B With a partner, practice speaking by asking and answering questions about the information in A.

Example **A** : Is Robert from America?
B : No, he isn't. He is from England.

Activity-2

A Listen to the recordings and check (✓) the correct boxes. 🎧

Questions	Thomas and Jane	Tyler and Diana	Minho and Sarah
1. Are they both from America?	Yes ☐ No ☐	Yes ☐ No ☐	Yes ☐ No ☐
2. Are they married?	Yes ☐ No ☐	Yes ☐ No ☐	Yes ☐ No ☐
3. Are they happy with each other?	Yes ☐ No ☐	Yes ☐ No ☐	Yes ☐ No ☐
4. Are they good at speaking Korean?	Yes ☐ No ☐	Yes ☐ No ☐	Yes ☐ No ☐
5. Are they in Korea now?	Yes ☐ No ☐	Yes ☐ No ☐	Yes ☐ No ☐

22 Unit 01 · Simple Present of *Be* verb

B With a partner, practice speaking by asking and answering questions about the information in A.

> Example
>
> **A** : Are Thomas and Jane both from America?
>
> **B** : No, they aren't. Thomas is from America. Jane is from Thailand.

Activity-3

A With a partner, practice speaking by taking turns asking and answering the following questions. Make sure to use complete sentences.

> Example
>
> **A** : Are you married?
>
> **B** : No, I'm not. I am single. / Yes, I am.

1. you / a student?

2. your favorite color / blue?

3. you / a morning person?

4. you / in love with someone?

5. your birthday / in December?

6. you / thirsty?

7. you / in your 20s?

8. you / shy?

9. your phone / expensive?

Activity - 4

A With a partner, practice speaking by asking and answering questions about Susan's weekly schedule.

1 / 1 Tue New Year's party (Hilton Hotel)	**1 / 2** Wed Helen's B-day party (Helen's)
1 / 3 Thu Lunch with Dona (Burger King)	**1 / 4** Fri Brother's wedding (Hyatt Hotel)
1 / 5 Sat Housewarming party (My house)	**1 / 6** Sun Gwen's baby shower (Gwen's)

weekly schedule

Example

A : When is the New Year's party?   **B** : It is on January 1st.

A : What day is it?   **B** : It's Tuesday.

A : Where is it?   **B** : It's at the Hilton Hotel.

Activity - 5

A Ask your partner the questions in the interview sheet and fill in the information.

Interview Sheet

1. What is your name? _____

2. How old are you? _____

3. Where are you from? _____

4. When is your birthday? _____

5. How tall are you? _____

6. What is your job? _____

7. What is your favorite food? _____

8. Who is your favorite movie star? _____

B Present the information about your partner to the class.

Example My partner's name is Chris. He is 27 years old. He is in his late 20s. He is from America. His birthday is July 5th. He is 175 cm tall. He is an office worker. His favorite food is pasta. His favorite movie star is Matt Damon.

Pronouns
대명사

PART 1 · I miss them so much.

Get Started

2-1. mp3

Read and listen to the dialogue.

Jonathan: Heather, who are **they** in that picture?

Heather: Oh, **they** are my high school friends, Claire and Phil. I miss **them** so much.

Jonathan: Where are **they** now?

Heather: Claire is in the U.S. now. **She** goes to college. Phil is in Singapore. **He** has his own business there. I want to visit **them** someday.

Jonathan: Do **you** talk to **them** often?

Heather: Yes. **We** usually chat online.

Jonathan: That's great. I hope to meet **them** someday.

Focus

▍대명사 (Pronouns)

● 대명사는 동일한 명사(사람, 사물)의 반복적인 사용을 피하기 위해 명사를 대신하여 쓰이는 품사입니다. 대명사는 명사의 역할을 그대로 수행하여 문장에서 주어, 목적어, 보어 자리에 사용됩니다.

Serena is from China. Serena loves Gary, and Gary loves Serena, too.
Serena and Gary are a happy couple.

→ Serena is from China. She loves Gary, and he loves Serena, too.
They are a happy couple.

1 주격 대명사 / 목적격 대명사 (Subject Pronouns / Object Pronouns)

		Subject Pronouns		Object Pronouns
Singular	I	I am from China.	me	You love **me**.
	you	**You** are from China.	you	He loves **you**.
	he	**He** is from China.	him	She loves **him**.
	she	**She** is from China.	her	He loves **her**.
	it	**It** is from China.	it	They love **it**.
Plural	we	**We** are from China.	us	People love **us**.
	you	**You** are from China.	you	They love **you**.
	they	**They** are from China.	them	My family loves **them**.

Exercise

A Change the nouns to subject pronouns.

Example   Mr. Smith ➡ ___he___

1. Ms. Gellar ➡ _____
2. Jane and Becky ➡ _____

3. police officers ➡ _____
4. a boy ➡ _____

5. James and Lisa ➡ _____
6. a cat ➡ _____

7. Eddie and Alex ➡ _____
8. Eddie and you ➡ _____

9. Eddie and I ➡ _____
10. students and a teacher ➡ _____

11. a book ➡ _____
12. books ➡ _____

13. Veronica ➡ _____
14. my family and I ➡ _____

B **Fill in the blanks with the correct subject pronouns.**

> Example   Julia didn't come to biology class. __She__ was sick all day.

1. Joe's party is on October 1st. _____ will be fun!

2. Carlos and Patricia are cousins. _____ are in England now.

3. My dad and I jog every morning. _____ like jogging together.

4. My classmates are really nice to me. _____ help me with my homework.

5. The capital of the Philippines is Manila. _____ is also a famous tourist spot.

6. John gave his pen to Mary. Now, _____ doesn't have it.

7. Sally and I already had breakfast because _____ got up early.

C **Rewrite the sentences by changing the underlined nouns to object pronouns.**

> Example   I lent my new sports car to my brother.
> ➡ _I lent my new sports car to him._

1. Ms. Gellar loves her children.

   ➡ _____

2. Jane wants to sell her computer.

   ➡ _____

3. The officer talked to my family and me.

   ➡ _____

4. Sally sent e-mails to some friends.

   ➡ _____

5. I'll put the photos on the wall.

   ➡ _____

6. He took his mom to a fancy restaurant.

   ➡ _____

D Change the underlined nouns to subject pronouns and object pronouns.

Example   Danni bought a coffee mug yesterday. _She_ used _it_ today.

1. Sarah has many friends. _____ all like _____.

2. Jimmy baked some cookies this morning. _____ will give _____ to Jen.

3. Lindsey doesn't like her classmates. So, _____ doesn't talk to _____ often.

4. Carrie has many old clothes. _____ wants to throw _____ away.

5. Robert likes the duo singers, 'B-stars'. _____ really wants to meet _____.

6. My grandparents gave some money to my sister and me. _____ are very nice to _____.

7. The little boy likes to play with his toy. _____ got _____ for his birthday.

E Find the errors in the use of pronouns and correct them.

Mr. Simpson and Mrs. Simpson got married 15 years ago. ~~Them~~ _They_ have two beautiful children, Joanna and Peter. They try to spend more time with they.

Joanna is 12 years old. Her just entered middle school. Her is always at the top of the class, and everybody likes she. She has lots of good friends. She sometimes invites they to her home and plays games together.

Peter is six years old. He goes to kindergarten. He can't go to school by himself, so Mrs. Simpson takes he there every morning. Him loves singing and dancing in front of his family and friends.

Get Started

2-2. mp3

Read and listen to the dialogue.

Jane: Is that dog **yours**?

Tim: No. That's not **mine**. My dog is over there, on the bench.

Jane: Which one? The small, white one?

Tim: Yes, that white Maltese is **mine**. Isn't he cute?

Jane: Yes, he is. Then whose dog is that?

Tim: It's my friend **Julie's**. The black dog is **hers**, too. I sometimes take care of **her** dogs.

Jane: You are very kind.

Focus

▌ 소유격 형용사 / 소유대명사 (Possessive Adjectives / Possessive Pronouns)

- 소유격 형용사는 '~의'란 의미로 명사와 함께 쓰이는 반면, 소유대명사는 '~의 것'이란 뜻으로 소유와 명사의 의미를 모두 포함하고 있어 뒤에 명사가 따라 나오지 않습니다.

	Possessive Adjectives		Possessive Pronouns	
Singular	**my**	This is **my** dog.	**mine**	This is **mine**.
	your	Is that **your** dog?	**yours**	Is that **yours**?
	his	It's **his** dog.	**his**	The dog is **his**.
	her	It's **her** cat.	**hers**	The cat is **hers**.
	its	The dog shakes **its** tail.	**(X)**	
Plural	**our**	This is **our** house.	**ours**	This is **ours**.
	your	Is that **your** house?	**yours**	Is that **yours**?
	their	It's **their** house.	**theirs**	It's **theirs**.

소유격 명사 / 소유대명사 (Possessive Nouns / Possessive Pronouns)

- 소유격 형용사와는 달리 명사를 직접 소유격으로 만드는 소유격 명사는 '~의'란 의미로 명사와 함께 쓰입니다.
- 소유대명사는 '~의 것'이란 뜻으로 소유격 명사와 형태는 똑같으나, 소유와 명사의 의미를 둘 다 포함하고 있으므로 명사와 함께 쓰이지 않습니다. 명사 뒤에 직접 이포스트로피와 −s('s), 혹은 어포스트로피(')만을 붙여 소유격 명사와 소유대명사를 만듭니다.
- s로 끝나지 않는 단수/복수 명사 뒤에는 어포스트로피와 −s('s) 를 붙입니다. boy's | Susan and Peter's | children's
- s로 끝나는 복수 명사 뒤에는 어포스트로피(') 만 붙입니다. boys' | girls' | babies'
- s로 끝나는 고유명사에는 어포스트로피만 붙이거나, 또는 어포스트로피와 −s('s)를 붙입니다. Chris' | Chris's

	Possessive Nouns		Possessive Pronouns	
Singular	Susan's	It's **Susan's** cat.	Susan's	The cat is **Susan's**.
	Chris's	It's **Chris's** cat.	Chris's	The cat is **Chris's**.
	dog's	That is my **dog's** toy.	dog's	That is my **dog's**.
Plural	Susan and Peter's	That's **Susan and Peter's** house.	Susan and Peter's	That's **Susan and Peter's**.
	girls'	They are my **girls'** toys.	girls'	They are my **girls'**.
	children's	They are my **children's** dolls.	children's	They are my **children's**.

Exercise

A Fill in the blanks with the correct possessive adjectives or possessive nouns.

> **Example** She found ___her___ watch under the table.

1. Fred is happy with _____ job.

2. That's (Tom) _____ motorcycle.

3. Mr. and Mrs. Jones are not living with _____ children now.

4. I forgot to bring _____ umbrella today. Can I borrow one of _____?

5. You went over the speed limit. Can I see _____ driver's license?

6. My wife and I are going to buy _____ own house next year.

7. The (students) _____ grades are emailed to their parents.

8. Ms. Berry is (Tom and Chris) _____ private tutor.

B Underline the possessive adjectives, triangle the possessive nouns, and circle the possessive pronouns in the sentences.

> **Example**   All the toys in △Andy's house are his (kids')

1. This is susan's cat. That's yours.

2. The best students in our school are Mr. Kelly's.

3. That is Cathy's phone. I'm sure it's hers.

4. These sketchbooks aren't mine. They're my children's.

5. Robin parks his car in this parking lot. The red car is his.

6. Sally's boyfriend bought her a necklace. That necklace is hers.

7. Today is our 2nd wedding anniversary. We will have dinner at my friend's restaurant.

8. That's not my car. That's my brother's. Mine is over there.

C Rewrite the sentences by changing the underlined words to possessive pronouns.

> **Example**   This is my pen. ➡ _This is mine_ .

1. Are those your books?

   ➡ _____

2. I didn't have an umbrella, so Mina lent me her umbrella.

   ➡ _____

3. The black one is his cat.

   ➡ _____

4. That isn't <u>our bus</u>.

   → _____

5. Is it <u>your cellphone</u>?

   → _____

6. The robots are my <u>children's toys</u>.

   → _____

7. Did you buy the paintings at <u>Claire's gallery</u>?

   → _____

8. It's their fault, not <u>our fault</u>.

   → _____

D **Circle the correct answers.**

Example This bag is (my /(mine)).

1. This table is (our / ours).

2. Fiona likes (hers / her) roommate.

3. It's none of (yours / your) business.

4. We hope for (their / theirs) happiness.

5. The elephant moves (it's / its) nose slowly.

6. The (boys' / boys's) tennis match is tomorrow.

7. They went to the movies with (their / theirs) co-workers.

8. (Sam and Sally's / Sam's and Sally's) wedding is on September 3rd.

Whose earrings are those?

Get Started

2-3. mp3

Read and listen to the dialogue.

Mike : Whose watch is **this**?

Alicia : I think it's Helen's. She lost her watch a few days ago in **this** room.

Mike : Oh, I see. There are also earrings under the couch. Whose earrings are **those**?

Alicia : Let me see. Oh, they are mine. I was wondering where they were.

Mike : I'm glad you found them. They look expensive.

Alicia : They are.

Focus

❚ 지시 대명사 (Demonstrative Pronouns)

● 지시 대명사는 사람이나 사물을 가리키는 대명사를 뜻합니다. 가까운 것을 가리킬 때는 this / these, 멀리 있는 것을 가리킬 때는 that / those을 사용합니다. this와 that은 단수의 사람이나 사물을 가리킬 때, these와 those는 둘 이상 복수의 사람이나 사물을 가리킬 때 사용합니다.

Singular		Plural	
This (이것)	Q : Whose book is **this**? A : It is Jane's.	**These** (이것들)	Q : Whose books are **these**? A : They are Jane's.
That (저것)	Q : Whose pencil is **that**? A : It is Peter's.	**Those** (저것들)	Q : Whose pencils are **those**? A : They are Peter's.

Exercise

Ⓐ **1. Fill in the blanks with *this / these*.**

1. _____ apple
2. _____ umbrellas
3. _____ university
4. _____ pictures
5. _____ desk
6. _____ socks

2. Fill in the blanks with *that* / *those*.

1. _____ horse 2. _____ restaurants 3. _____ bicycle
4. _____ children 5. _____ house 6. _____ women

B Change the underlined words to singular forms or plural forms.

> **Example** This is a wooden chair. ➡ <u>These are</u> wooden chairs.

1. <u>That is a rabbit</u> under the table. ➡ _____ rabbits under the table.

2. <u>Those are</u> nice wedding dresses. ➡ _____ a nice wedding dress.

3. <u>These letters are</u> for you. ➡ _____ for you.

4. <u>That is a</u> nice restaurant. ➡ _____ nice restaurants.

5. <u>This red umbrella is</u> Jane's. ➡ _____ Jane's.

6. <u>These are</u> from China. ➡ _____ from China.

7. <u>Those apples are</u> not for eating. ➡ _____ not for eating.

C Answer the following questions as the questions are answered in the example.

> **Example** Is this your book? ➡ <u>No, it's not. That is my book.</u>
>
> Are those your boots? ➡ <u>No, they're not. These are my boots.</u>

1. Is that a squirrel? ➡ _____.

2. Is this your toothbrush? ➡ _____.

3. Are these your pants? ➡ _____.

4. Are those your earrings? ➡ _____.

5. Is that yours? ➡ _____.

6. Are these your sister's? ➡ _____.

D Use the words given to make questions. Then, look at the pictures and write the answers.

| Example | cups → | Whose cups are these? | They are Clare's. |

1. books ⇒ _____ _____

2. cellphones ⇒ _____ _____

3. flower vase ⇒ _____ _____

4. laptop ⇒ _____ _____

5. clock ⇒ _____ _____

6. picture frame ⇒ _____ _____

PART 4   It is snowing outside.

Get Started 🎧

2-4. mp3

Read and listen to the dialogue.

Alex: Hurry up, Kristin.

Kristin: Why? What time is **it**?

Alex: **It's** already 8:10. We have to be at the airport by 9:30.

Kristin: How long does **it** take to get to the airport?

Alex: It's a one-hour bus ride.

Kristin: Then we still have enough time. Don't worry.

Alex: But **it's** snowing outside. The traffic will be bad.
      Please hurry up.

Focus

▌ 비인칭 주어 it (Impersonal Pronoun 'it')

● 비인칭 주어 it은 아무런 뜻은 없으나 시간, 날짜, 날씨, 기온, 거리를 나타내는 문장을 만드는데 있어 주어 역할을 하는 필수 요소입니다.

Time	Date	Weather	Temperature	Distance

Q: What time is **it** now?	Q: What date is **it** today?	Q: How is the weather today?	Q: What's the temperature today?	Q: How far is **it** to the bank?
A: **It's** 7 am.	A: **It's** September 15th.	A: **It's** rainy.	A: **It's** 40°C.	A: **It's** a three-minute walk from here.

Exercise

(A) Match the questions with the correct answers.

1. How's the weather today? •   • a. It's January 29th.

2. What time is it now? •   • b. It's a five-minute walk from here.

3. How far is it to the library? •   • c. It's 20°C today.

4. What date is it today? •   • d. It's foggy and cold.

5. What's the temperature today? •   • e. It's Tuesday.

6. What day is it today? •   • f. It's almost 8.

(B) Look at the pictures and write questions and answers.

Example

Q: How's the weather today?

A: It's windy.

1. **Q:** _____?

   A: _____.

2. **Q:** _____?

   A: _____.

3. Q: _____?

A: _____.

4. Q: _____?

A: _____.

C Read the sentences. Write 'S' if it is a subject pronoun, write 'O' if it is an object pronoun, and write 'I' if it is an impersonal pronoun.

> Example It's an apple.   S

1. What time is it?   _____

2. He told me about it.   _____

3. It's seven fifteen.   _____

4. Dwayne took it with him.   _____

5. It is made in China.   _____

6. It is a ten-minute bus ride from here.   _____

7. The movie was great. It was fun.   _____

8. It rains a lot in tropical countries.   _____

9. They didn't really enjoy it.   _____

10. It's November 15th.   _____

Let's Speak!

Activity - 1

A With a partner, practice using pronouns in a conversation.

- calculator
- Fiona's
- add these numbers

- phone
- my brother's
- check my voice messages

- digital camera
- my cousin's
- take just one shot

Example
Jesse: Could I borrow _your pen_ for a moment?
Rachel: Oh, it's not _my pen_. It's _Andy's_.
Jesse: I just need to _fill out this form_.
Rachel: Then could you give it back to _him_ later?
Jesse: Of course, I will.

Activity - 2

A 1. Listen to the story about Tom's family and write the correct names in the boxes.

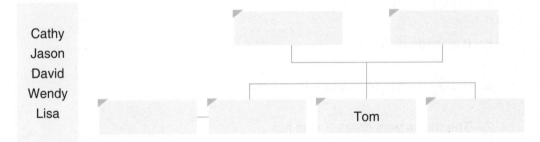

Cathy
Jason
David
Wendy
Lisa

Tom

2. With a partner, take turns saying how the people in the family tree above are related.

Example Tom is Wendy's brother.

B **1.** Look at the picture and listen to the story about Tom's family again. Find whom the items in the picture belong to. Write the names of the people in the correct boxes in the picture.

Tom

2. With a partner, practice speaking by asking and answering questions about the picture above.

Example   **A:** Is this Wendy's digital camera?   **B:** No, it's not hers.

               A: Then, whose digital camera is this?   **B:** It's Tom's.

Activity - 3

A Student A

With a partner, complete the table by asking each other questions about the current time and weather in the cities in the chart.

City	Date & Time	Weather
New York	10 / 7 08:00 pm	Sunny
Chicago		
Los Angeles	10 / 7 05:00 pm	Windy
Brasilia		
Sydney	10 / 8 11:00 am	Rainy
Paris		
Tokyo	10 / 8 10:00 am	Windy
Bangkok		
Beijing	10 / 8 09:00 am	Foggy
Moscow		
London	10 / 8 01:00 am	Rainy

Example
A : What time is it in Chicago? ⇒ B : It's 7 o'clock in the evening.
A : Is it the 7th? ⇒ B : Yes, it is.
A : What's the weather like? ⇒ B : It's cold.

B Student B

With a partner, complete the table by asking each other questions about the current time and weather in the cities in the chart.

City	Date & Time	Weather
New York		
Chicago	10 / 7 07:00 pm	Cold
Los Angeles		
Brasilia	10 / 7 10:00 pm	Cloudy
Sydney		
Paris	10 / 8 02:00 am	Sunny
Tokyo		
Bangkok	10 / 8 08:00 am	Hot
Beijing		
Moscow	10 / 8 04:00 am	Cloudy
London		

Example
B : What time is it in New York? → **A** : It's 8 o'clock in the evening.
B : Is it the 8th? → **A** : No, it isn't. It's the 7th.
B : What's the weather like? → **A** : It's sunny.

UNIT 03

Simple Present
현재시제

 Get Started

3-1. mp3

Read and listen to the passage.

My husband Tim and I **come** from Australia. **We teach** children at an international school in Korea. **Tim teaches** science, and **I teach** English. **I teach** my students with games, and **Tim takes** his class on field trips. **We love** our students, and **they love** us, too. **Tim doesn't plan** to go back to Australia. **I don't want** to leave either. **We love** our jobs.

Focus

▌ 일반동사의 현재시제 (Simple Present Tense)

- 현재시제는 현재의 동작이나 상태, 일반적인 사실, 혹은 습관이나 반복적인 행동을 나타낼 때 사용합니다.

1. 긍정문 / 부정문 (Affirmative Statements / Negative Statements)

	Subject	Verb		Subject (3rd person singular)	Verb	
Affirmative	I / You / We / They	**like**	apples.	He / She / It	**likes**	apples.

- 부정문의 경우, do not / does not 을 사용해 [주어 + do not / does not + 동사원형]의 순으로 문장을 만듭니다.

	Subject	Verb		Subject	Verb	
Negative	I / You / We / They	**do not like** (=don't like)	apples.	He / She / It	**does not like** (=doesn't like)	apples.

More Examples

Affirmative	Negative
We **brush** our teeth after lunch.	We **don't brush** our teeth after lunch.
Tom **washes** his hands before lunch.	Tom **doesn't wash** his hands before lunch.
Jasmine **studies** English every day.	Jasmine **doesn't study** English every day.

▌주어가 3인칭 단수일 때 일반동사의 형태

● 동사원형에 -s를 붙이는 것이 일반적이나, 일반적으로 다음의 규칙에 따라 형태가 달라집니다.

Rules		Examples	Pronunciation
일반 동사: **-s**	clean → **cleans** get → **gets**	He **cleans** the classroom. She **gets** home early.	• 유성음, 모음으로 끝나는 동사: [z] • 무성음([k],[t],[p],[f],[θ])으로 끝나는 동사: [s]
-sh, -ch, -x, -z, -s로 끝나는 동사: **-es**	watch → **watches** fix → **fixes**	Tom **watches** TV a lot. Sally **fixes** computers.	[iz]
자음 + y로 끝나는 동사: **y → i + -es**	carry → **carries**	She **carries** a big bag.	[z]
모음 + y로 끝나는 동사: **-s**	play → **plays**	The dog **plays** with a cat.	[z]
불규칙 동사	go → **goes** do → **does** have → **has**	He **goes** to school. Gwen **does** yoga. She **has** two sisters.	[z]

Exercise

(A) 1. Fill in the blanks with the correct simple present forms of the verbs given.

Example   Jennifer (watch) __watches__ TV every night.

1. The dog (swim) _____ in the lake.

2. She (dress) _____ all in pink for parties.

3. Scott always (work) _____ in his office until 9 pm.

4. Sally always (finish) _____ her paper on time.

5. My cousin (draw) _____ pictures very well.

6. Allison (sleep) _____ in on Sunday mornings.

7. My younger brother sometimes (play) _____ soccer with his friends.

2. Circle the correct pronunciation of the endings of the verbs that you wrote above.

Example   watches   [s]   ([z])   [iz]

1. [s]   [z]   [iz]   2. [s]   [z]   [iz]

3. [s]   [z]   [iz]   4. [s]   [z]   [iz]

5. [s]   [z]   [iz]   6. [s]   [z]   [iz]

7. [s]   [z]   [iz]

(B) Correct the errors in the sentences.

Example   She miss her boyfriend very much.
              misses

1. Carrie do her homework after dinner.

2. My child have a toothache.

3. Peter carrys his laptop everywhere.

4. My dog Chocho bark every night.

5. Sally and Albert goes to an amusement park on weekends.

6. Mel don't wear make-up.

7. He do not plays winter sports, but he love summer sports.

C Fill in the blanks with the correct negative forms of the verbs given. Use the simple present tense.

Example   Jane (speak) __doesn't speak__ four languages.

1. He (pay) _____ the rent every month.

2. We (have) _____ enough money for a party.

3. The bird (fly) _____ high up in the sky.

4. The children (watch) _____ TV these days.

5. Freddy (do) _____ his homework sometimes.

6. Jane (wash) _____ her hair in the morning.

D Complete the passage by using the correct simple present forms of the verbs given.

I (live) _____ with my roommate. His name is Ken. He is a night owl, but I am an early bird. I usually (go) _____ to bed before midnight and (wake up) _____ at 6 am. However, Ken (go) _____ to bed around 2 or 3 in the morning. He sometimes (party) _____ until 6 am. Then he (come) _____ back home and (sleep) _____. All my classes (start) _____ early, but Ken always (go) _____ to school after lunch. We don't (have) _____ anything in common, but we (get) _____ along well.

Get Started

3-2. mp3

Read and listen to the dialogue.

Ray: You look exhausted, Cathy.

Cathy: I have so much stress these days.

Ray: How come?

Cathy: It's because of my manager.

Ray: **Does he give** you a hard time?

Cathy: **No, he doesn't.** But he gives me a lot of work. So I
      have to work late often.

Ray: I'm sorry to hear that.

Cathy: What about you, Ray? **Do you feel** stressed at work?

Ray: **No, I don't.** I really enjoy working here.

Focus

▌현재시제 의문문 (Yes/No Questions and Short Answers)

- 일반동사가 포함된 현재시제 의문문은 조동사 do/does를 주어 앞에 놓아 [Do/Does + 주어 + 동사원형…?]의 어순으로 만듭니다.

Yes/No Questions			Short Answers			
Do/Does	Subject	Base Verb	Affirmative		Negative	
Do	**I** **you** **we** **they**	get up early? live in a city? drink coffee often?	**Yes,**	you **do**. I/we **do**. you/we **do**. they **do**. he/she/it **does**.	**No,**	you **don't**. I/we **don't**. you/we **don't**. they **don't**. he/she/it **doesn't**.
Does	**she** **he** **it**	drive a car? work hard? make sense?				

축약형: do not = don't ▌ does not = doesn't

Exercise

A Look at the pictures and complete the questions and answers in the simple present tense by using the proper words from the box.

read	clean her room	eat meat
wash the dishes	argue	exercise

Example

Q: _Does_ he _wash the dishes_
every day?
A: No, _he doesn't_.

1.

Q: _____ your sister _____
every day?
A: Yes, _____.

2.

Q: _____ he _____ a lot?
A: No, _____.

3.

Q: _____ they _____ often?
A: Yes, _____.

4.

Q: _____ she _____ a lot?
A: No, _____.

5.

Q: _____ she _____ ?
A: No, _____.

B Use the words given to make yes/no questions in the simple present tense. Then, complete the short answers.

> **Example** Kelly / play / baseball after school
>
> ➡ <u>Does Kelly play baseball after school?</u>　<u>No, she doesn't.</u>

1. Alex / always sleep late

   ➡ _____ ?　No, _____

2. Sarah / wash / her clothes on Saturdays

   ➡ _____ ?　Yes, _____

3. your baby / cry / all night

   ➡ _____ ?　No, _____

4. your sister / help you / with your homework

   ➡ _____ ?　Yes, _____

5. you / need / the car today

   ➡ _____ ?　No, _____

6. they / go to the movies every weekend

   ➡ _____ ?　Yes, _____

Where do you teach?

Get Started

3-3. mp3

Read and listen to the dialogue.

James: Nice to meet you. I'm James.

Tina: I'm Tina. It's nice to meet you, too.

James: So, **how do you feel** today?

Tina: Not bad. What about you?

James: I'm a little nervous. So, **what do you do**?

Tina: I'm a math teacher.

James: Wow. **Where do you teach?**

Tina: I teach at North Point High School.

James: I heard it's a great school. Anyway, I think we should order. **What do you want to have**?

Tina: Well, I don't eat meat, so I'll get some salads.

Focus

▌ 현재시제 Wh- 의문문 (Wh-Questions and Short Answers)

● Wh- 의문문은 Wh- 의문사를 do / does 앞에 놓아 [Wh- 의문사 + 조동사 do / does + 주어 + 동사 …?]의 어순으로 만듭니다.

Wh- word	Do	Subject	Verb	Wh- word	Does	Subject (3rd person singular)	Verb
Where	**do**	you	live?	**Where**	**does**	she / he / it	live?

More Examples

Wh- Questions	Short Answers
Where do you live?	In Nashville.
What do you do after school / work?	I go to a yoga class.
When does your father go to work?	At 7:30.
How does she feel?	She feels alright.
Who do you like?	Jenny.
Why does he like Jenny?	Because she is kind.

Exercise

(A) Match the questions with the most appropriate answers and write the correct answer letters in the blanks.

Questions	Answers
_____ 1. When does he exercise?	a. Downtown.
_____ 2. Who does she live with?	b. Because they have a lot of work.
_____ 3. What do you think about him?	c. He's a doctor.
_____ 4. Why do they work late every day?	d. Usually at night.
_____ 5. Where does this bus go?	e. I go to the gym.
_____ 6. How do I look today?	f. With her cousin.
_____ 7. What does his father do?	g. You look nice in that suit.
_____ 8. What do you usually do after work?	h. I think he's kind.

(B) Put the words in the correct order to make questions. Then, write your own short answers.

> **Example** date / who / these days / you / do
> → **Q:** Who do you date these days?   **A:** Helen.

1. does / the laptop / how / work
   → **Q:** _____? **A:** _____

2. Freddy / work / does / where
   → **Q:** _____? **A:** _____

3. I / job / my / when / start / do
   → **Q:** _____? **A:** _____

4. sister / do / your / what / does

   → Q: _____? A: _____

5. does / he / the book / why / like

   → Q: _____? A: _____

6. do / you / what / on weekends / do

   → Q: _____? A: _____

C The people are doing an interview. Complete the questions in the dialogue by using the information given by the interviewee.

Interviewer: _Where do you live?_

Interviewee: I live in Granville.

Interviewer: _____ live with?

Interviewee: I live with my parents and brother.

Interviewer: Where _____?

Interviewee: My father works at a bank, and my mother works at an elementary school.

Interviewer: _____ do?

Interviewee: My brother is a reporter.

Interviewer: Why _____ want to work for this company?

Interviewee: Because I can learn many things about magazines.

Let's Speak!

Activity-1

Ⓐ Listen to the recordings and fill in the chart. 🎧

	1	**2**	**3**
Name	Nora	Clare	Eric
Country			
Occupation			
Likes			
Dislikes			
Activities after work / school			

B Fill in the chart with your own information. Then, with a partner, take turns reading the information to each other and fill in your partner's answers.

	You	Your Partner
Name		
Country		
Occupation		
Likes		
Dislikes		
Activities after work / school		

Activity - 2

(A) Listen to Ray and Cathy, and check (√) the correct boxes. 🎧

Does he / she ...	Ray	Cathy
... get stressed easily?	Yes ☐ No ☐	Yes ☐ No ☐
... exercise regularly?	Yes ☐ No ☐	Yes ☐ No ☐
... eat breakfast every day?	Yes ☐ No ☐	Yes ☐ No ☐

(B) This questionnaire is to test how stressed you are. Answer the questions on your own. Then, ask your partner the questions and check (√) your partner's answers.

Do you...	You	Partner
... enjoy your work or school life?	Yes ☐ No ☐	Yes ☐ No ☐
... dress up every day?	Yes ☐ No ☐	Yes ☐ No ☐
... go to work or school early?	Yes ☐ No ☐	Yes ☐ No ☐
... get along well with your co-workers or friends	Yes ☐ No ☐	Yes ☐ No ☐
... live with your family?	Yes ☐ No ☐	Yes ☐ No ☐
... get to work or school on time?	Yes ☐ No ☐	Yes ☐ No ☐
... watch your favorite show often?	Yes ☐ No ☐	Yes ☐ No ☐
... spend time with friends regularly?	Yes ☐ No ☐	Yes ☐ No ☐

☞ 7-8 yes: Low stress | 4-6 yes: Moderate stress | 0-3 yes: High stress

(C) Present the result of the questionnaire to the class.

> Example   I enjoy my work, but my partner doesn't enjoy his work.

Activity - 3

(A) Listen to the recording about James and fill in the blanks. Then, listen again to check the answers.

Q1: _____?

A1: He lives in New York City.

Q2: _____?

A2: He is a web designer.

Q3: _____?

A3: He works at an online game company.

Q4: _____ every morning?

A4: He studies Chinese.

Q5: _____?

A5: They think he is nice and clever.

Q6: _____?

A6: He usually goes to the gym.

Q7: What does he do after he gets home?

A7: _____.

(B) With a partner, practice speaking by taking turns asking and answering the questions from A. Use the simple present tense.

Example   **A:** Where do you live?
          B: I live in Los Angeles.

Nouns & Articles
명사와 관사

PART 1

Bring a hat and sunglasses.

Get Started 🎧

4-1. mp3

Read and listen to the dialogue.

Mark: What are these for?

Rachel: I'm packing for a **hike** tomorrow.

Mark: Oh, I see.

Rachel: What should I bring?

Mark: Bring a **hat** and **sunglasses**. Don't forget a **towel**, too.

Rachel: How about an **umbrella**?

Mark: Umm, a **raincoat** will be better.

Rachel: That's a good **idea**. Thanks.

Focus

▌명사 (Nouns)

- 명사는 셀 수 있는 명사(count noun)와 셀 수 없는 명사(non-count noun)로 구분됩니다.
- 셀 수 있는 명사(count noun)가 단수로 쓰일 때는 단수 명사라고 하며, 단수 명사 앞에는 부정관사(a/an)를 반드시 붙여야 합니다. 또한 복수로 쓰일 때는 복수 명사라고 하며 끝에 -s/-es가 붙습니다.

1. 단수 명사 (Singular Nouns)

자음으로 시작하는 단수 명사	a	book, cat, pencil, phone, watch, university...
모음 (/a/,/e/,/i/,/o/,/u/)으로 시작하는 단수 명사	an	apple, elephant, example, engineer, umbrella, hour...

There is a book on the table. | She doesn't have an umbrella.

> 모음으로 시작하는 단어라도, 발음상 [u]가 아닌 [ju] 일 경우에는 부정관사 a를 씁니다.

a university(대학교)　**a** union member(노조원)

자음으로 시작하는 단어라도, 발음상 자음이 아닌 모음일 경우에는 부정관사 an을 씁니다.

an hour(한 시간)　**an** honest man(정직한 사람)　**an** LCD screen(LCD 스크린)

2 규칙 복수 명사 (Regular Plural Nouns)

● 명사 자체에 -s / -es를 붙여서 복수형을 만들 수 있는 명사

Rules	Examples	
대부분의 명사: -s	a cat → two cat**s** a computer → four computer**s**	a book → three book**s**
-s, -ch, -sh, -z, -x로 끝나는 명사: -es	a box → two box**es** a class → five class**es**	a dish → four dish**es** a church → three church**es**
-f, -fe로 끝나는 명사: -f, -fe → -ves	a knife → many kni**ves** ※예외: roof**s**, cliff**s**, chef**s**	a leaf → some lea**ves**
자음 + o로 끝나는 명사: -es	a potato → three potato**es** ※예외: piano**s**, avocado**s**, photo**s**	a tomato → four tomato**es**
모음 + o로 끝나는 명사: -s	a video → many video**s**	a radio → two radio**s**
자음 + y로 끝나는 명사: -y → -ies	a lily → lil**ies**	a story → stor**ies**
모음 + y로 끝나는 명사: -s	a toy → many toy**s**	a boy → four boy**s**

You need some potato**es**, tomato**es**, and avocados.

I will write two short stor**ies** today.　Hanna has many toys.

3 불규칙 복수 명사 (Irregular Plural Nouns)

● 별도로 존재하는 복수형을 사용하여야 하는 명사

Rules	Examples		
단수 / 복수 형태가 같은 명사	a fish → many fish a sheep → ten sheep	a deer → two deer	
단수 / 복수 형태가 다른 명사	a mouse → two mice a tooth → many teeth a man → two men a child → many children	a goose → two geese a foot → two feet a woman → two women	
항상 복수형을 사용하는 명사	pants pajamas	jeans glasses	scissors clothes

She is married and has two children.　　I bought jeans and pajamas at a flea market.

Exercise

A Fill in the blanks with *a / an*.

> Example   a   pencil

1. _____ clock
2. _____ apple
3. _____ FBI agent
4. _____ wall
5. _____ universe
6. _____ example
7. _____ hour
8. _____ bottle
9. _____ engineer
10. _____ child
11. _____ university
12. _____ house
13. _____ MVP
14. _____ candy

B Fill in the blanks with *a / an*.

> Example   Tina works in _an_ office.

1. She carries _____ suitcase everywhere.

2. Dean always wears _____ hat.

3. Sally is _____ university student.

4. My uncle lives in _____ apartment.

5. It takes about _____ hour to get to the airport.

6. He is _____ MBA student.

7. She is _____ pretty girl.

8. Erin doesn't have _____ umbrella.

C Write the correct singular or plural forms of the following words.

Example   watch   _watches_

1. box   _____
2. _____   animals
3. _____   lilies
4. story   _____
5. piano   _____
6. fish   _____
7. mouse   _____
8. photo   _____
9. _____   teeth
10. roof   _____
11. child   _____
12. sheep   _____

D Rewrite the sentences by changing the underlined singular nouns to plural nouns. Use the proper forms of the verbs.

Example   A dog is a faithful animal. ➡ _Dogs are faithful animals._

1. We bought an umbrella.   ➡ _____

2. An apple falls from a tree.   ➡ _____

3. There is a book on the table.   ➡ _____

4. I bought a peach and a banana.   ➡ _____

5. A cat is a good pet.   ➡ _____

6. A photographer takes a photo.   ➡ _____

7. There is an elephant in the zoo.   ➡ _____

Get Started 🎧

4-2. mp3

Read and listen to the dialogue.

Aaron: Christine, do you know how to bake?

Christine: Sure.

Aaron: I want to bake **some cupcakes** for my girlfriend.

Christine: That's very sweet of you!

Aaron: Well, I was wondering if you could help me.

Christine: Of course! Do you have all of the ingredients?

Aaron: What do I need?

Christine: You need **some butter**, **two cups of sugar**, **four eggs**, **two teaspoons of baking powder**, and **three cups of flour**.

Aaron: Hold on, let me write that down.

Focus

▌셀 수 없는 명사 (Non-count Nouns)

● 셀 수 없는 명사는 다음과 같이 분류됩니다.

집합명사 (Collective Nouns)	각각의 사물을 하나로 보는 집합체 형식을 띤 명사
	a chair, a desk, a table → **furniture** an apple, strawberries, a watermelon → **fruit** vegetables, potatoes, spaghetti → **food** a bus, a car, a truck → **traffic** nickels, dimes, dollars → **money**
물질명사 (Material Nouns)	형체는 있으나, 용기에 따라 모양이 달라지거나 하는 액체, 기체와 같은 명사
	paper, butter, cheese, water, coffee, tea, milk, air, smoke, sugar, flour, rice
추상명사 (Abstract Nouns)	구체적인 형체가 없이 추상적인 개념을 나타내는 명사
	information, intelligence, love, happiness, beauty, knowledge, advice, experience, kindness
과목 이름 (Subjects of Study)	학문이나 학과 이름을 나타내는 명사
	Education, Geography, Grammar, Mathematics, Economics, Politics
기타	weather, climate, rain, sunshine

셀 수 없는 명사의 수량을 나타내는 법 (Quantifiers for Non-count Nouns)

		Singular	Plural		Singular	Plural
By Container		a bottle of water	two bottles of water		a cup of coffee	six cups of coffee
		a carton of milk	three cartons of milk		a glass of water	seven glasses of water
		a jar of pickles	four jars of pickles		a bowl of soup	eight bowls of soup
		a bag of flour	five bags of flour		a tube of toothpaste	two tubes of toothpaste
By Portion		a piece of paper	two pieces of paper		a slice of pizza	five slices of pizza
		a piece of cake	four pieces of cake		a scoop of ice cream	six scoops of ice cream
By Measure-ment		a teaspoon of oil	two teaspoons of oil		a gallon of juice	ten gallons of juice
Others		a loaf of bread	two loaves of bread		a piece of advice	two pieces of advice
		a bar of soap	four bars of soap		a piece of furniture	three pieces of furniture

Exercise

A Put the following nouns in the correct categories.

Example	furniture	apple	telephone	money	vegetable
	rice	flower	information	tooth	bread
	knowledge	girl	computer	pencil	traffic
	food	book	coffee	T-shirt	dollar
	advice	word	air	happiness	

Count Nouns

_____   _____
_____   _____
_____   _____
_____   _____
_____   _____

Non-Count Nouns

_____   _____
_____   _____
_____   _____
_____   _____
_____   _____

B Match the non-count nouns with appropriate quantifiers.

1. water   • a. a scoop of

2. jam   • b. a glass of

3. bread   • c. a cup of

4. ice cream   • d. a jar of

5. furniture   • e. a loaf of

6. coffee   • f. a piece of

7. soap   • g. a bottle of

8. soup   • h. a bar of

9. wine   • i. a bowl of

C Correct the errors in the sentences.

Example   Jane drinks eight waters a day.
                    ∧
              glasses of

1. I have many furnitures in my room.

2. Could you give me some advices?

3. He needs an information about the event.

4. I am so tired. I really need some coffees.

5. I don't have many hairs.

6. She usually eats two bowl of rices.

7. She majors in an Economics.

8. Can I have two loaf of bread, please?

Get Started 🎧

4-3. mp3

Read and listen to the dialogue.

Chelsea: I think cats are sweet animals. What do you think?

Nick: Yes, I agree.

Chelsea: I really want to get a cat these days.

Nick: What kind of cat do you want?

Chelsea: I want a striped cat.

Nick: Oh, I saw a cat like that in the local animal shelter. It had orange and white stripes.

Chelsea: Really? How can I adopt the cat?

Nick: I'm not sure about the process. Let's go to the shelter together and find it out!

Focus

▌부정관사(a/an)와 정관사(the)

1 부정관사: a/an

• a/an은 셀 수 있는 명사 중 단수 명사 앞에 놓여 다음과 같은 의미를 나타냅니다.

　① 하나를 의미(one)   I need a pencil.

　② 매~/각각~ 을 의미(per)   I do yoga once a week.

　③ 불특정다수 중에 하나를 의미(any)   She has a smartphone.

　④ 그룹 전체를 총칭하는 의미(as a whole group)   A dog is a lovely pet. 개는 사랑스런 애완동물이다.

2 정관사: the

• 셀 수 있는 명사 혹은 셀 수 없는 명사 모두 앞에 놓여 다음과 같이 사용됩니다.

　① 앞에서 이미 언급한 것을 다시 언급할 때(mentioned before)

　 I made spaghetti last night.   Where is the spaghetti?

　② 특정한 것을 지칭할 때(specific object)

　 I usually sit at the desk.

　③ 정황상 어떤 것을 지칭하는지 분명할 때(clear from the situation)

　 Please close the door.

　④ 유일한 존재나 sky, Sun, sea 등과 같은 자연환경 관련 단어 앞에

　 The hotel is by the sea.

Exercise

(A) Look at the pictures and fill in the blanks in the passage with *a* / *an* / *the*.

Tim thinks _____ dog is a lovely pet. He loves dogs. He adopted _____ puppy yesterday. He has three puppies at home. Tim feeds _____ puppies three times _____ day.

Every Friday is _____ special day for _____ puppies. Tim usually gives them a bath. _____ puppy with white fur runs away every time before _____ bath time. After the bath, he takes them to _____ park.

(B) Fill in the blanks with *a* / *an* / *the*.

1. Q. How did you get to school?   A. I took _____ taxi.

2. Q. Can I borrow _____ pen?   A. Sure, I have many.

3. Q. I feel sick.   A. Why don't you see _____ doctor?

4. Q. Do you have a part-time job?   A. Yes, I work as _____ server.

5. Q. Can I get you anything?   A. Yes, I'll have _____ glass of water.

6. Q. What would you like?   A. I'd like _____ donut, please.

7. _____ apple _____ day keeps the doctor away.

8. _____ evening dress in the closet is very beautiful.

Ⓒ Complete the dialogues by using *a* / *an* / *the*.

1. **Helen**: Tony, here is _____ package for you.

   Tony: Really? Who is it from?

   Helen: I'm not sure, but it says _____ package is from Belgium.

   Tony: Belgium? Oh, then that's from my uncle. He owns _____ chocolate shop in Belgium.

2. **Cory**: What do you want to do today?

   Emily: I want to see _____ movie.

   Cory: What movie do you want to watch?

   Emily: _____ one with the superheroes. I don't know _____ title of this movie.

   Cory: Oh, you mean *Ultra Force*? Where do you want to see _____ film?

   Emily: I know _____ movie theater downtown. It has _____ huge screen and _____ good sound system. _____ theater is called Max.

   Cory: Okay. I'll reserve _____ tickets.

Get Started 🎧

4-4. mp3

Read and listen to the dialogue.

Dustin : There is **some coffee** in the coffee maker. Help yourself.

Mary : Oh, thank you, Dustin. Do you drink **a lot of coffee**?

Dustin : No, not really. How about you?

Mary : Oh, I drink **a lot of coffee** with **lots of cookies**. Are there **any cookies** here?

Dustin : I'm sorry. There aren't **any cookies** left.

Focus

some / any

- some / any는 'a(an)' 또는 'the'와 같이 명사 앞에 위치하며, 복수 명사 또는 셀 수 없는 명사 앞에서 '몇몇의, 약간의'라는 뜻으로 쓰입니다. some은 긍정문에만 쓰이고, any는 부정문 / 의문문에서 사용합니다.

	셀 수 있는 복수 명사 앞	셀 수 없는 명사 앞
긍정문 **some**	There are **some** apples in the basket.	There is **some** coffee in the coffee maker.
부정문 **any**	There are not (=aren't) **any** apples in the basket.	There is not (=isn't) **any** coffee in the coffee maker.
의문문 **any**	Are there **any** apples in the basket?	Is there **any** coffee in the coffee maker?

many / a lot of

- many / a lot of는 복수 명사 앞에서 '많은'이란 뜻으로 쓰입니다.

There are <u>many</u> apples.

There are <u>a lot of</u> (=lots of) apples.

Are there <u>many</u> (=a lot of) apples?

→ Yes, there are.

▌ much / a lot of

● much / a lot of는 셀 수 없는 명사 앞에서 '많은'이란 뜻으로 쓰입니다.

There is much information.

There is a lot of (=lots of) information.

Is there much (=a lot of) information?

→ Yes, there is.

Exercise

Ⓐ Circle the correct answers.

> **Example**   I didn't cook (some / ⓐny) dinner.

1. There aren't (some / any) hospitals near my house.

2. Is there (some / any) homework for tomorrow?

3. There is (some / any) orange juice in the fridge.

4. I ate (some / any) apples for a snack.

5. Do you read (some / any) of Shakespeare's dramas?

6. I didn't have (some / any) time, so I couldn't go to her party.

7. Did you write (some / any) essays in English?

B Fill in the blanks with *many/much*.

> `Example` I have too __much__ homework this evening.

1. Are there _____ students in your class?

2. Julie doesn't eat _____ rice. She is on a diet.

3. There are _____ socks in the drawer.

4. There is _____ information about aliens on the Internet.

5. Don't put too _____ salt in your food. It's not good for your health.

C Correct the errors in the sentences.

> `Example` He doesn't have ~~some~~ free time these days.
>   any

1. Is there some jam in the refrigerator?

2. There are much bananas.

3. I invited much friends to my birthday party.

4. I'm so full. I ate too many bread.

5. I'm writing a paper. I need many information.

Let's Speak!

Activity - 1

A With a partner, practice speaking by asking and answering questions.

| Example | **A :** Is there a / an [단수 명사] in the classroom?
 B : Yes, there is.
 No, there isn't. | **A :** Are there (any) [복수 명사] in the classroom?
 B : Yes, there are (some) [복수 명사].
 No, there aren't any [복수 명사]. |

B Listen to the recordings and write the numbers of the descriptions in the correct boxes in the picture above. 🎧

C Think of some countable objects in your bedroom. Then, with a partner, practice speaking by asking and answering questions about the objects.

| Example | **A :** Is there a TV in your bedroom?
 B : Yes, there is **a TV**. Are there **any windows** in your bedroom?
 A : No, there aren't **any windows**. |

Activity-2

A Imagine this is your refrigerator at home.

These are the items that you have in the refrigerator. Circle the count nouns and underline the non-count nouns in the box.

| apple | strawberry jam | milk | cherry | cake |
| orange juice | lemon | carrot | cucumber | |

B With a partner, practice speaking by asking and answering questions about the items in the refrigerator. Use only the quantifiers from page 63.

> Example
> **A**: How many pieces of cake are there in the refrigerator?
> **B**: There are **two pieces of cake** in the refrigerator.

C Do the same activity as B. This time, use only *many / much / a lot of / some*.

> Example
> **A**: Is there **any cake** in the refrigerator?
> **B**: There is **some cake** in the refrigerator.

UNIT 05

Present Progressive

현재진행시제

Get Started

5-1. mp3

Read and listen to the passage.

Dear Crystal,

How is everything going? I am writing to you on the train to Mountain Jungfrau. It's snowing on the top of the mountain, but the weather is nice. I am doing great here in Switzerland. I'm studying tourism. I'm also working part time, so I'm learning about many new things. Anyway, are you doing OK with the new job? I miss you a lot. I will write you another e-mail soon.

Lots of love,

Lena

Focus

▌현재진행시제 (Present Progressive Tense)

● 현재진행시제는 현재 말하고 있는 시점에서 일어나고 있는 어떤 일이나 상태에 대해 말할 때 사용됩니다. 현재 진행시제 문장에서 동사는 현재진행형 [be + 동사 –ing]의 형태이며 '~하는 중이다'라는 의미를 전달합니다.

1. 동사의 –ing형 만들기 규칙

Rules	Examples
모음 + 자음으로 끝날 경우: 마지막 자음 추가 + -ing	sit → sitting run → running
두 개의 모음 + 자음으로 끝날 경우: -ing	train → training eat → eating
자음 + e로 끝날 경우: e 삭제 + -ing	type → typing have → having
그 외 대부분의 동사: -ing	read → reading wash → washing

2 현재진행시제의 긍정문 (Affirmative Statements)

Subject	Present progressive form		Subject	Present progressive form	
I	am	singing.	We / Tom and I	are	having lunch.
You	are	driving fast.	You / You and Tom	are	doing well.
He / She / It	is	hanging around.	They	are	working at the office.

> 회화에서 현재 진행시제 문장을 말할 때는 주로 주어와 be 동사를 축약하여 말합니다.
>
> I am= I'm ∥ He / She / It is = He's / She's / It's ∥ You / We / They are = You're / We're / They're

3 현재진행시제의 부정문 (Negative Statements)

Subject	Present progressive - negative form		Subject	Present progressive - negative form	
I	am not	singing.	We / Tom and I	are not	having lunch.
You	are not	driving fast.	You / You and Tom	are not	doing well.
He / She / It	is not	hanging around.	They	are not	working at the office.

> 부정문에서 축약형을 사용할 때는 주어와 be동사를 축약하는 방법과 be 동사와 not을 축약하는 방법이 있습니다.
>
> He's not singing. = He isn't singing.

Exercise

A Change the verbs into the *-ing* forms.

Example   do ➡ _doing_

1. feel	➡ _____		2. take	➡ _____
3. stop	➡ _____		4. plan	➡ _____
5. rain	➡ _____		6. fix	➡ _____
7. come	➡ _____		8. sleep	➡ _____
9. carry	➡ _____		10. shine	➡ _____
11. think	➡ _____		12. tan	➡ _____
13. watch	➡ _____		14. smile	➡ _____
15. wait	➡ _____		16. agree	➡ _____
17. use	➡ _____		18. prefer	➡ _____
19. play	➡ _____		20. pay	➡ _____

B Complete the sentences by describing what is happening in each picture.

Example   1.   2.   3.

fall   shine   study   watch

4.   5.   6.   7.

run   polish   wear   shake

Example   Leaves _are falling_ from the tree.

1. The Sun _____.

2. Tom and Jane _____ in the library.

3. People _____ a movie in the cinema.

4. Fiona _____ on the ground.

5. He _____ his shoes.

6. The man _____ a sweater.

7. They _____ hands.

Ⓒ **Change the affirmative statements into negative statements.**

Example   I am reading a novel. ➡ _I am not reading a novel._

1. She is riding her bicycle.   ➡ _____

2. Victoria is having lunch with friends.   ➡ _____

3. She is waiting for the bus now.   ➡ _____

4. The students are playing soccer.   ➡ _____

5. Susan and I are swimming in the pool.   ➡ _____

6. They are talking on the phone right now.   ➡ _____

7. James is carrying his suitcase on the plane. ➡ _____

D Complete the passage with the present progressive forms of the verbs given.

Today is Monday. It is 8:30 in the morning. People are already at work.

Some people (make) _____ coffee and some people (eat)

_____ breakfast in the cafeteria. In the office, I (read)

_____ a newspaper. Some people (check) _____

their e-mails. The manager (talk) _____ to her assistant.

Peter (carry) _____ some copies of a report.

Ryan (talk) _____ on the phone. Jesse (work) _____

_____ at her computer. Tony and Susie (have) _____

a meeting. Everyone (get) _____ ready for the first day of

the week. I hope this week goes well.

PART 2   Are you seeing anyone?

Get Started

5-2. mp3

Read and listen to the dialogue.

Amy: Hi, Pam. What are you doing here?

Pam: I'm waiting for my boyfriend. How about you?

Amy: **I'm just window shopping.**

Pam: I see. By the way, **are you seeing** anyone these days?

Amy: **Yes, I am.**

Pam: Tell me all about him!

Focus

▌현재진행시제의 Yes / No 의문문

- [be 동사 + 주어 + 동사 –ing…?] 어순으로 be 동사가 주어 앞에 위치합니다.

Yes / No Questions			Short Answers	
Be Verb	Subject	Verb-ing	Affirmative	Negative
Am	I	**talking** too fast?	Yes, **you are**.	No, **you are not**.
Are	you	**listening** to me?	Yes, **I am**.	No, **I am not**.
Is	he / she / it	**watching** TV?	Yes, **he / she / it is**.	No, **he / she / it is not**.
Are	you / they	**having** dinner?	Yes, **we / they are**.	No, **we / they are not**.

Exercise

A Complete the questions in the present progressive tense by using the verbs given. Then, complete the short answers.

> **Example** **Q:** ___Are___ you ___enjoying___ the party?
> **A:** No, ___I'm not___ .

1. (have) **Q:** _____ John _____ lunch with Stacy?
   A: Yes, _____ .

2. (work) **Q:** _____ they _____ in the office?
   A: No, _____ .

3. (talk) **Q:** _____ I _____ too fast?
   A: No, _____ .

4. (wear) **Q:** _____ he _____ a blue sweater?
   A: Yes, _____ .

5. (study) **Q:** _____ you guys _____ for the exam?
   A: Yes, _____ .

6. (make) **Q:** _____ she _____ dinner now?
   A: No, _____ .

7. (take) **Q:** _____ you _____ the yoga class?
   A: Yes, _____ .

8. (see) **Q:** _____ you _____ anyone?
   A: Yes, _____ .

9. (take) **Q:** _____ she _____ pictures of her children?
   A: No, _____ .

10. (wait) **Q:** _____ they _____ for their turn?
    A: Yes, _____ .

B Use the words given to make yes / no questions in the present progressive tense. Then, complete the short answers. When you answer 'No', add your own words.

Example Derrick / watch TV

➡ ___Is Derrick watching TV?___ No, ___he isn't. He's reading a book.___

1. Gary and Eric / play golf

   ➡ _____? No, _____

2. they / look for their car

   ➡ _____? No, _____

3. the manager / go over the report

   ➡ _____? Yes, _____

4. Ms. Lee / do the laundry

   ➡ _____? Yes, _____

5. the boss / come now

   ➡ _____? No, _____

6. he / take a walk in the park

   ➡ _____? No, _____

7. the baby / look at the baby mobile

   ➡ _____? Yes, _____

8. she / wear a black suit

   ➡ _____? Yes, _____

9. you / write a letter

   ➡ _____? Yes, _____

10. they / talk about me

   ➡ _____? No, _____

Get Started

5-3. mp3

Read and listen to the dialogue.

Sam : Where are you now?

Linda : I'm in the library.

Sam : What are you doing there at this late hour?

Linda : I'm studying for the exam tomorrow.

Sam : Who are you studying with?

Linda : I'm studying with Robert and Phil. Are you at home?

Sam : Yeah, I'm getting some rest.

Focus

▌현재진행시제의 Wh- 의문문 (Wh- Questions and Short Answers)

● [Wh- 의문사 + be 동사 + 주어 + 동사 -ing …?] 어순으로 만들어지며, 문장의 제일 앞에 의문사가 위치하고 그 이하는 Yes / No 의문문과 같은 형태입니다.

Wh- word	Be Verb	Subject	Verb -ing	Answers
What	are	you	**looking** at?	**I'm looking** at the sky.
Who	is	he / she	**talking** to?	He / She **is talking** to Sam.
Where	are	we	**going**?	We**'re going** to the gym.
Why	are	they	**making** a cake?	Because today is Tina's birthday.
How	is	he	**doing**?	He **is doing** great.

Exercise

(A) Put the words in the correct order to make questions. Then, choose the correct answer choices and write the answers in complete sentences.

Example   is / who / talking to / he   ➡   _Who is he talking to?_

     a. an apple   b. his professor   c. to the bank

➡ _He's talking to his professor._

1. she / where / sitting / is   ➡ _____?
   a. at the front row   b. with her mother   c. at school

   ➡ _____

2. what / you / doing / are   ➡ _____?
   a. Saturday night   b. the bathroom   c. clean the room

   ➡ _____

3. are / you and Gary / how / these days / doing   ➡ _____?
   a. subway   b. fine   c. sleepy

   ➡ _____

4. why / he / yawning / is   ➡ _____?
   a. feel tired   b. have a good time   c. take a bath

   ➡ _____

5. with / they / who / are / having dinner   ➡ _____?
   a. salad and steak   b. their classmates   c. Indian restaurant

   ➡ _____

6. he / what / fixing / is   ➡ _____?
   a. the dog   b. phone call   c. a motorcycle

   ➡ _____

7. are / the people / where / now / singing   ➡ _____?
   a. on the street   b. rocker   c. rap music

   ➡ _____

B Find the errors and correct them.

Example   Where is Danni and Andy going?   He's going to school.
             are   They're

1. How are he doing?   He are doing well.

2. When is she playing with?   She's playing with her toy.

3. Why are you read this book?   Because I'm studying this author.

4. What are they playing tennis with?   They're playing tennis with Jason.

5. What is Sally do now?   She studies for the exam.

C Complete the dialogues by using proper wh- words and the present progressive forms of the verbs given.

1. Ian: _____ are you (go) _____ now?

    Lisa: I'm (go) _____ to the supermarket. How about you?

    Ian: I'm (wait for) _____ Chris. He's on his way here now.

2. Travis: Hey, _____ are you (do) _____?

    Stacey: I'm (chat) _____ online.

    Travis: _____ are you (talk to) _____?

    Stacey: Brian.

3. **Lisa**:   Hello.

Austin: Hello. This is Austin. _____ are you (do) _____?

Lisa: Oh, hi! I'm just (watch) _____ TV at home.

Austin: How is the weather in New Jersey?

Lisa: Hmm... It's (snow) _____. My kids (make) _____

snowmen and (have) _____ a snowball fight.

Austin: Oh, I see. How are you (feel) _____ these days?

Lisa: I'm (feel) _____ better. I'm (exercise) _____ these

days.

Austin: Good. Take care. I'll call you later. Bye.

Let's Speak!

Activity-1

A Look around the classroom and see what the people are doing. Check the things that are happening now.

- Somebody's checking his / her text messages.
- Somebody's coming into the classroom.
- Somebody's walking around.
- Somebody's chewing gum.
- Somebody's writing on the book.
- Somebody's yawning.
- Somebody's having coffee.
- Somebody's smiling.
- Somebody's writing on the board.
- Somebody's scratching his / her head.

What else is happening in the classroom now?

- _____
- _____
- _____

B With a partner, practice speaking by asking and answering questions about the information in A. Use the present progressive tense.

Example
A: Is anybody checking text messages?
B: Yes. Susan is checking her text messages. / No. Nobody is checking text messages.

Activity-2

A Look at the pictures and write sentences in the present progressive tense. You may use the words from the box.

It is raining now.

rain   walk   run   hold an umbrella   share an umbrella

A man is sitting on a chair.

sit on a chair   use a laptop   wear
drink coffee   read a newspaper   carry a tray

Activity-3

A Listen to the following people's messages on Emily voicemail and check (✓)
if the following statements are true or false. 🎧

		True	False
Daisy	1. Daisy is listening to music at home.	☐	☐
	2. It's raining outside today.	☐	☐
	3. Daisy is not working today.	☐	☐
Tim	1. Tim is calling Emily from Fiji.	☐	☐
	2. Tim is enjoying his vacation a lot.	☐	☐
	3. People are dancing at the beach.	☐	☐
Eunice	1. Eunice is at the amusement park with Julia.	☐	☐
	2. They are watching the parade.	☐	☐
	3. Eunice wants to come again with Emily.	☐	☐

B With a partner, compare the answers and practice speaking by asking and
answering questions about the information in A. Use the present progressive
tense.

> **Example**
> **A:** Is Daisy listening to music at home?
> **B:** No. She's reading comic books at home.

Activity-4

A With a partner, look at the picture and practice speaking by asking and answering questions about what the people are doing. Use the present progressive tense and the words from the box.

ask questions to a salesperson	stand in front of a mirror
talk on the phone	run to his mom
pay with his credit card	carry a purse

Example **A** : What is David doing?

B : He is paying with his credit card.

UNIT 06

Simple Past of *Be* verb

Be동사의 과거시제

Get Started 🎧

Read and listen to the passage.

6-1. mp3

I'm Mark. I had my first part-time job when I **was** 18. I **was** a high school student then. I **was** a paper delivery person for six months. **The work was** stressful. Every day, I **was** at work at 5 am. **My manager wasn't** very kind to me. I **was** very tired after work, but I **was** happy with the job. **It was** a good experience for me.

Focus

Be 동사의 과거시제 (Past Tense of *Be* Verb)

● Be 동사가 들어간 문장에서는 be 동사의 과거형을 사용하여 과거시제를 나타냅니다. am/is의 과거형은 was, are의 과거형은 were입니다.

1 Be 동사 과거시제의 긍정문 (Affirmative Statements)

Singular			Plural		
Subject	**Be Verb**		**Subject**	**Be Verb**	
I	**was**	tired last night.	We / Tom and I	**were**	friends before.
You	**were**	late yesterday.	You / You and Tom	**were**	28 last year.
He / She	**was**	at the movies last night.	They / Tom and Tina	**were**	there last week.
It / The peach	**was**	fresh and sweet.	The books	**were**	in the bookcase.
There	**was**	a man in the room.	There	**were**	many people outside.

2 Be동사 과거시제의 부정문 (Negative Statements)

● not을 be 동사의 과거형 was와 were 뒤에 붙여서 부정문을 만듭니다.

Singular			Plural		
I **was not**		tired last night.	We **were not**		friends before.
You **were not**		late yesterday.	You **were not**		28 last year.
He / She **was not**		at the movies last night.			there last week.
It **was not**		fresh and sweet.	They **were not**		
There **was not**		a man in the room.	There **were not**		many people outside.

> Be 동사 과거시제 부정문에서는 be 동사와 not의 축약형이 자주 쓰입니다. was not과 were not은 각각 wasn't, weren't로 축약될 수 있습니다.
>
> I / He / She / It / There **was not** = I / He / She / It / There **wasn't**
> You / We / They / There **were not** = You / We / They / There **weren't**

Exercise

(A) Fill in the blanks with the correct simple past forms of *be* verbs.

> Example   Mindy ___was___ upset yesterday.

1. He _____ a salesperson at the store.

2. Tim _____ still in bed at 10 am this morning.

3. You _____ late for work yesterday.

4. There _____ many visitors in the museum.

5. We _____ glad to see you again.

6. I _____ in Singapore last year.

7. There _____ only one student in the class.

8. Dorothy and I _____ at the party last night.

B Rewrite the sentences using contracted forms.

> **Example** The teacher was not happy with Ryan's work.
>
> ➡ _The teacher wasn't happy with Ryan's work._

1. Jane was not at school yesterday.

   ➡ _____

2. It was not sunny this morning.

   ➡ _____

3. This backpack was not expensive.

   ➡ _____

4. Danny and Sarah were not in Paris a few months ago.

   ➡ _____

5. They were not at work last Friday.

   ➡ _____

6. Travis was not at the movies with Gina last night.

   ➡ _____

C Put the words in the correct order to make complete sentences.

> **Example** cloudy / it / yesterday / was ➡ _It was cloudy yesterday._

1. nervous / was / during / I / the speech

   ➡ _____

2. were / on / they / vacation / in / Fiji

   ➡ _____

3. mad / Sue / wasn't / at her brother / this morning

   ➡ _____

4. not / were / the shoes / expensive

➡ _____

5. excited / very / people / were / at the concert

➡ _____

6. wasn't / the food / good / at the buffet

➡ _____

(D) **Fill in the blanks with the correct simple present and simple past forms of *be* verbs. Use the negative forms where needed.**

Example   Jason __wasn't__ home yesterday afternoon. He __was__ in the library.

1. That book _____ in the bookcase before. Now it _____ under the table.

2. I _____ very tired yesterday, but I _____ fine today.

3. We _____ in our mid 20s ten years ago. Now we _____ in our mid 30s.

4. You _____ at the bank at 3 o'clock yesterday, right? I saw you there.

5. He _____ from New Zealand, but he _____ born in Australia.

6. The weather _____ great yesterday, but today it _____ raining.

7. Suzie and Mark _____ in the meeting room this morning. Where _____ they this morning?

8. Claire and I _____ at the carnival last weekend. The fireworks _____ wonderful.

How was the seminar yesterday?

Get Started 🎧

6-2. mp3

Read and listen to the dialogue.

Ruby: Hey, Sean. **How was** the seminar yesterday?

Sean: Oh, it was alright.

Ruby: **Were** there many people in the audience?

Sean: **Yes, there were.** It was a bit crowded, but it was OK.

Ruby: **What was** the topic of the seminar?

Sean: It was about recycling.

Ruby: Oh, I see. **Was** the seminar in Wilson Hall?

Sean: **Yes, it was.** Come to the next seminar. It's next
Tuesday.

Focus

▌ Be 동사 과거시제의 의문문 (Yes/No Questions and Short Answers)

● [Was/Were + 주어 …?]의 형태로 be 동사의 과거형을 주어 앞에 두어 의문문을 만듭니다.

Yes / No Questions			Short Answers	
Be Verb	**Subject**		**Affirmative**	**Negative**
Was	I	too loud?	Yes, you were.	No, you were not.
Were	you	in Chicago last March?	Yes, I was.	No, I was not.
Was	he / she / it	OK yesterday?	Yes, he / she / it was.	No, he / she / it was not.
Were	we / you / they	on time?	Yes, you / we / they were.	No, you / we / they were not.

> 의문문에 대한 긍정의 답변에서는 축약형을 사용하지 않고, 부정을 나타내는 답변에서만 축약형을 사용할 수
> 있습니다.
>
> No, I wasn't. | No, they weren't.

Be 동사 과거시제의 Wh- 의문문 (Wh- Questions and Short Answers)

- [Wh- 의문사 + was / were + 주어 …?]의 형태로 의문문을 만듭니다.

Wh-word	Be Verb	Subject …?	Answers
Where	was	I last night?	You were at the party.
Who	were	you with last night?	I was with my friends.
When	was	the meeting?	It was at 3 o'clock yesterday.
How	was	the seminar last night?	It was informative.
What	were	the students like?	They were nice and hardworking.
How old	were	the students?	They were about 20 years old.

Exercise

A Circle the correct words and complete the answers.

Questions	Answers
1. (Was / Were) you late for class yesterday?	No, I _____.
2. (Was / Were) your hair long before?	Yes, it _____.
3. (Where / When / Who) was your birthday?	It _____ the day before yesterday.
4. (Where / How / When) were you and Jason last night?	We _____ at the movies.
5. (Where / What / How) was the baseball game yesterday?	It _____ fantastic.
6. (Were / Was) they excited about the news?	Yes, they _____.
7. (Who / Where / What) was the weather like yesterday?	It _____ sunny and hot.
8. (Who / How / What) was the host of the show?	It _____ Linda Jones.

B Complete the questions and answers using proper wh- words and simple past forms of *be* verbs. Then match the questions with the correct answers.

Questions	Answers

1. _____ the food good at that restaurant?

2. _____ the concert fun?

3. _____ I happy yesterday?

4. _____ Patty and June friends before?

5. Where _____ you born?

6. _____ was the wedding?

7. _____ was the weather in London yesterday?

8. _____ was this rope for?

a. Yes, you _____.

b. I _____ born in Seoul.

c. Yes, it _____ good but very expensive.

d. No, it _____.

e. It _____ for climbing mountains.

f. It _____ rainy all day yesterday.

g. They _____, but not anymore.

h. It _____ yesterday afternoon.

ⓒ Complete the dialogues by using proper wh- words and simple past forms of *be* verbs.

1. **Jamie:** Hey, I called you several times last week, but you _____
   home. _____ were you?

   Mindy: Oh, I _____ at my grandmother's. She _____ sick, so I
   took care of her. Anyway, why did you call me?

   Jamie: Actually, I had my birthday party last week.

   Mindy: Really? When _____ your birthday?

   Jamie: It _____ last Friday. Many people _____ at the party.

   Mindy: Oh, I'm sorry that I couldn't make it.

2. **Stephen:** Monica, _____ was the concert last night?

   Monica: It _____ OK. I enjoyed it, but the music _____ so loud.

   Stephen: _____ it crowded with many people?

   Monica: Yeah, Many people _____ there.

   Stephen: _____ Pete and Kelly there, too?

   Monica: No, they _____. They _____ at work.

   Stephen: _____ time _____ the concert?

   Monica: It started at 7:30 pm.

   Stephen: _____ was it?

   Monica: It was at the Civic Art Center.

3. **Sue:** _____ you and Ben at the meeting?

   Fred: No, we _____.

   Sue: Then _____ _____ you guys?

   Fred: We _____ with our clients at the restaurant. Actually, we didn't
   know about the meeting. _____ _____ it?

   Sue: It _____ at 1:30. The information _____ on the bulletin
   board.

   Fred: Oh, we didn't check it. What _____ it about?

   Sue: It _____ about sales reports.

6-3. mp3

Activity-1

A With a partner, practice speaking by asking and answering questions about each picture. Use the simple past tense and the words given.

1.

11:00 pm

you

2.

03:00 pm

Dorothy

3.

09:00 am

you and Tom

4.

01:30 pm

Sarah and Jane

5.

08:20 pm

Chris

6.

10:00 am

Jessica

Example

A: _Were you_ **at home** _at 5 o'clock_ yesterday?

B: No, _I wasn't_ .

A: Then where _were you_ at that time?

B: _I was at the concert_ .

Activity-2

(A) Look at the attendance sheet of an English class, and complete the answers to the following questions.

Attendance Sheet

Present: ○   Late: △   Absent: ×

		11 / 1 Mon	11 / 2 Tue	11 / 3 Wed	11 / 4 Thu	11 / 5 Fri
1	Albert	○	○	○	○	○
2	Brian	○	○	○	△	× (on vacation)
3	Cathy	△	○	× (sick)	○	× (on vacation)
4	Dana	× (sick)	△	○	× (busy)	○
5	Eric	△	○	× (busy)	○	○

Example **Q**: Who was present for the whole week?
A: Albert **was** present for the whole week.

Q: Who was absent on Monday?
A: _____

Q: Why was the person absent on Monday?
A: _____

Q: Who was late on November 4th?
A: _____

(B) With a partner, take turns asking and answering other questions about the attendance sheet.

Activity - 3

(A) Listen to people talking about their first jobs and fill in the chart. Then, with a partner, compare your answers by asking each other the questions about the people. 🎧

My First Job

	Rosa	Aaron	Tina
How old was she / he then?			
What was the job?			
How was the work?			
Was it a good experience?			

B Do you remember your first day at work? Fill in the chart with your own information. Then, with a partner, take turns asking the questions to each other and fill in your partner's answers.

	You	Your Partner
How old were you then?		
What was the job?		
How was the work?		
Was it a good experience?		

UNIT 07

Simple Past
과거시제

Get Started 🎧

Read and listen to the dialogue.

7-1. mp3

Laura: What **did** you do on the weekend, Rob?

Rob: **My girlfriend and I went** to a jazz festival.

Laura: Wow! Tell me about it.

Rob: Well, **I drove** for an hour to get there. **My girlfriend brought** sandwiches and some fruits. **The festival was** an outdoor event, so **we sat down** on the grass and **watched** the performances. **All of the jazz artists played** very well. **We took** many pictures and **enjoyed** ourselves.

Laura: Sounds like **you had** a great time!

Rob: **We did!**

Focus

▎과거시제 (Simple Past Tense)

● 과거시제는 과거에 있었던 일에 대해 말할 때 사용되며, 동사의 과거형(past form)을 사용해 표현합니다. 동사의 과거형은 동사원형에 -(e)d 를 붙이는 형태와 고유의 과거형이 있는 형태로 나뉩니다. 동사 원형 + -(e)d로 과거형이 만들어지는 동사를 규칙동사(Regular Verbs)라고 하고, 고유의 과거형을 갖는 동사를 불규칙 동사 (Irregular Verbs)라고 합니다.

1. 동사의 과거형

① 규칙동사(Regular Verbs)의 경우

Rules		Examples	
대부분의 동사: -ed		finish → finish**ed**	work → work**ed**
-e로 끝난 동사: -d		smile → smile**d**	arrive → arrive**d**
[자음 + 모음 + 자음]으로 끝난 동사: 마지막 자음 덧붙임 + -ed		stop → stop**ped**	omit → omit**ted**
[자음 + y]로 끝난 동사: -y → -i + -ed		carry → carr**ied**	study → stud**ied**
[모음 + y]로 끝난 동사: -ed		play → play**ed**	enjoy → enjoy**ed**

② 불규칙 동사(Irregular Verbs)의 경우

Base Verb	Past Form	Base Verb	Past Form	Base Verb	Past Form
begin	began	find	found	run	ran
bring	brought	fly	flew	say	said
buy	bought	forget	forgot	see	saw
catch	caught	get	got	sing	sang
choose	chose	give	gave	sit	sat
come	came	go	went	sleep	slept
cut	cut	have	had	speak	spoke
draw	drew	know	knew	stand	stood
drink	drank	leave	left	swim	swam
drive	drove	make	made	take	took
eat	ate	meet	met	tell	told
fall	fell	pay	paid	think	thought
fight	fought	ride	rode	write	wrote

2. 과거시제의 긍정문 / 부정문 (Affirmative Statements / Negative Statements)

과거시제의 부정문은 동사 원형 앞에 do의 과거형 did와 not을 사용해 [주어 + did not + 동사원형 …] 형태로 만들며, 이때 did not은 didn't로 축약될 수 있습니다.

Affirmative			Negative			
Subject	Verb(past form)		Subject	did not(didn't)	Base Verb	
I / You / He / She / It We / They	watched	TV yesterday.	I / You / He / She / It We / They	**did not (didn't)**	watch	TV yesterday.

3 과거를 나타내는 시간 표현

● 과거시제는 주로 다음과 같은 과거를 나타내는 시간 표현과 함께 사용됩니다.

yesterday	yesterday afternoon	a week ago	a month ago
before	in the past	in 2018	last night
last week	last month	last year	last Sunday

He **finished** the work yesterday.　　　　They **were** very popular in 2010.

Exercise

Ⓐ Change the verbs into the correct simple past forms.

Example　work ➡ _worked_

1. do   ➡ _____　　2. help   ➡ _____

3. bring   ➡ _____　　4. stop   ➡ _____

5. drink   ➡ _____　　6. think   ➡ _____

7. play   ➡ _____　　8. buy   ➡ _____

9. arrive   ➡ _____　　10. study   ➡ _____

11. go   ➡ _____　　12. have   ➡ _____

13. carry   ➡ _____　　14. open   ➡ _____

15. find   ➡ _____　　16. make   ➡ _____

17. show   ➡ _____　　18. drive   ➡ _____

19. stand   ➡ _____　　20. forget ➡ _____

B Fill in the blanks with correct simple past forms of the verbs given.

> Example This morning, he (exercise) _exercised_ in the park.

1. Last night, she (watch) _____ a movie.

2. Last Friday, Cliff (do) _____ the laundry.

3. Yesterday morning, he (go) _____ to work at 8 am.

4. Yesterday, he (eat) _____ a lot for lunch.

5. Jason (fall) _____ asleep during the meeting this afternoon.

6. Fiona (meet) _____ Jody at the party. It was a week ago.

7. Jack (finish) _____ his work last Sunday.

8. David likes to practice the violin. He (practice) _____ almost 8 hours yesterday.

C Change the affirmative statements into negative statements.

> Example I drove to work yesterday. ➡ _I didn't drive to work yesterday._

1. I finished my report yesterday.   ➡ _____

2. We enjoyed our vacation in Fiji.   ➡ _____

3. I went to the gym yesterday.   ➡ _____

4. They ate hamburgers for lunch.   ➡ _____

5. Julia came to my house yesterday.   ➡ _____

6. Carrie wrote an e-mail to her friend.   ➡ _____

7. She took her car to the garage.   ➡ _____

D Look at the pictures and using the words given, make affirmative or negative sentences in the simple past tense.

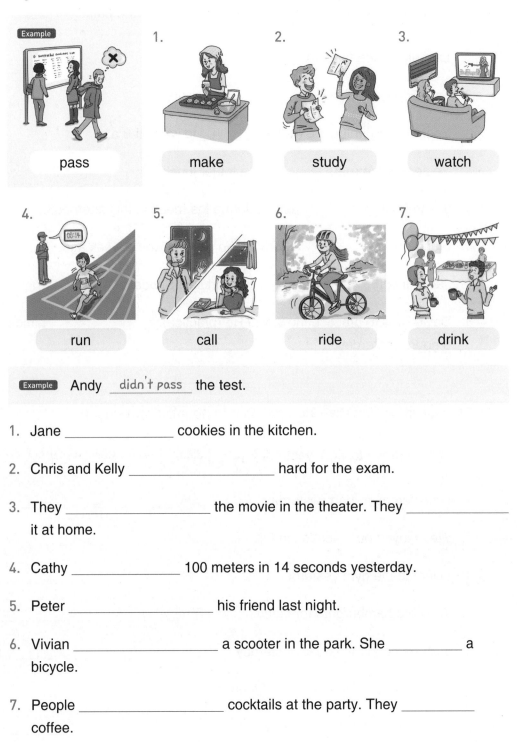

Example
pass

1. make

2. study

3. watch

4. run

5. call

6. ride

7. drink

Example   Andy _didn't pass_ the test.

1. Jane _____ cookies in the kitchen.

2. Chris and Kelly _____ hard for the exam.

3. They _____ the movie in the theater. They _____ it at home.

4. Cathy _____ 100 meters in 14 seconds yesterday.

5. Peter _____ his friend last night.

6. Vivian _____ a scooter in the park. She _____ a bicycle.

7. People _____ cocktails at the party. They _____ coffee.

E Complete the journal by filling in the blanks with the correct simple past forms of the verbs from the box.

Example   prepare   go   meet   make   chat   come   have   finish

December 4, Tuesday

I _____ a really busy day today! In the morning, I _____ a presentation for a business conference. Then I _____ my friends during lunch time. We _____ for an hour. After I _____ back to the office, I _____ my presentation. A lot of people were there. I was nervous, but I _____ the presentation successfully. Later in the afternoon, my co-workers and I _____ to a bar for some beer.

et Started

7-2. mp3

Read and listen to the dialogue.

Brian : How was the blind date yesterday? **Did it go** well?

Julia : Hmm. I'm not really sure.

Brian : Why? **Did he call** you after you got home?

Julia : **Yes, he did.**

Brian : Then, what was the problem?

Julia : Well, we didn't have much in common. So we didn't really talk much.

Brian : That's too bad.

Focus

▌ 과거시제의 Yes / No 의문문 (Yes / No Questions and Short Answers)

- 과거시제의 의문문은 [Did + 주어 + 동사원형 …?]의 형태로 만듭니다.

Yes / No Questions				Short Answers			
Did	**Subject**	**Base Verb**			**Affirmative**		**Negative**
Did	I / you / he / she / it / we / they	watch	TV yesterday?	**Yes,**	I / you / he / she / it we / they	**did. No,**	I / you / he / she / it we / they **didn't.**

Exercise

A Put the words in the correct order to make questions. Then, complete the short answers.

Example Tom / attend / did / the meeting / ? / No

➡ **Q**: _Did Tom attend the meeting?_   **A**: _No, he didn't._

1. they / did / to / go / the wedding / ? / Yes

   ➡ Q: _____   A: _____

2. find / you / did / the wallet / ? / No

   ➡ Q: _____   A: _____

3. get off / she / did / from work / ? / Yes

   ➡ Q: _____   A: _____

4. all of them / travel / did / Europe / to / ? / No

   ➡ Q: _____   A: _____

5. she / all day / work / yesterday / did / ? / Yes

   ➡ Q: _____   A: _____

6. enjoy / did / the movie / you / ? / Yes

   ➡ Q: _____   A: _____

7. stay / Sarah / home / did / ? / No

   ➡ Q: _____   A: _____

B Correct the errors in the questions and rewrite them.

Example Does the elevator worked yesterday?

     Did   work   ➡ _Did the elevator work yesterday?_

1. Did they went home early last night?   ➡ _____

2. Does she make pancakes last weekend?   ➡ _____

3. Did you arrived in New York this morning? ➡ _____

4. Ron and Darren handed in their papers? ➡ _____

5. Does your family move to the U.S. in 2015? ➡ _____

6. They stayed late at the office yesterday? ➡ _____

ⓒ **Change the sentences into yes / no questions. Then, write short answers.**

> **Example**   Jane drove her car downtown yesterday.
>
> ➡ **Q:** _Did Jane drive her car downtown yesterday?_   **A:** _Yes, she did._

1. She finally found a better job.

   ➡ **Q:** _____   **A:** _____

   _____

2. He and his friends caught the flu at the same time.

   ➡ **Q:** _____   **A:** _____

   _____

3. Mary got a birthday present from her husband.

   ➡ **Q:** _____   **A:** _____

   _____

4. Sasha and Mario didn't get home early last night.

   ➡ **Q:** _____   **A:** _____

   _____

5. Chandler didn't take his family to the resort last weekend.

   ➡ **Q:** _____   **A:** _____

   _____

6. They didn't have lunch with the president.

    → Q: _____   A: _____

         _____

7. My co-workers helped me a lot with the project.

    → Q: _____   A: _____

         _____

(D) **Complete the dialogues in the simple past tense by using the verbs given.**

1. **Jane:**   Katie, _____ you (meet) _____ Jerry last night?

    Katie: No, I _____. My boss (give) _____ me a lot of work

              yesterday, so I (stay) _____ late at the office.

    Jane: Oh, that's a shame.

2. **Melissa:**   _____ you (have) _____ a nice weekend?

    James: Yes, I did. I (go) _____ to see a musical.

    Melissa: Wow, how was it?

    James: It was fantastic! I really (love) _____ it.

3. **Ashley:**   _____ you (call) _____ me last night?

    Brian: Yes, I _____, but you (not answer) _____

              the phone.

    Ashley: I (be) _____ at our company dinner.

    Brian: What did you have?

    Ashley: I (have) _____ Chinese food.

    Brian: Oh, I see. _____ you (have) _____ a good time?

    Ashley: Yes. I _____.

Get Started

7-3 mp3

Read and listen to the dialogue.

Jack:	Vicky, **where did you go** for lunch?
Vicky:	I went to an Italian restaurant.
Jack:	**Who did you go** with?
Vicky:	With some coworkers.
Jack:	**What did you have** there?
Vicky:	I had some pizza and pasta.
Jack:	Sounds delicious.
Vicky:	Let's go together next time.

Focus

▌ 과거시제의 Wh- 의문문 (Wh- Questions and Short Answers)

● 과거시제의 Wh- 의문문은 [Wh- 의문사 + did + 주어 + 동사원형 …?]의 형태로 만듭니다.

Wh-word	did	Subject	Base Verb	Answers
What		I	miss?	You missed nothing.
Who		you	meet?	I met my friend.
When		he / she / it	leave?	He / she / It left a few minutes ago.
How	did	we	play at the concert?	You played very well.
Where		you	go?	We went to the public library.
Why		they	miss the class?	Because they had an important family event.
What time		you	get up this morning?	I got up at 6 this morning.

Exercise

(A) Complete the wh- questions in the simple past tense by using the information in the answers.

1. Q: (   ) (   ) you (   ) from the grocery store?
    A: I bought some tangerines.

2. Q: (   ) (   ) he (   ) me?
    A: He called you a few minutes ago.

3. Q: (   ) (   ) they (   ) with?
    A: They sat with their family.

4. Q: (   ) (   ) she (   ) before?
    A: She lived in Greenwich Village before.

5. Q: (   ) (   ) you (   ) there?
    A: I went there by bus.

6. Q: (   ) (   ) the manager (   ) at you?
    A: She yelled at me because I didn't meet the deadline.

7. Q: (   ) (   ) Tim (   ) back?
    A: He came back last Friday.

8. Q: (   ) (   ) you guys (   ) about?
    A: We talked about the travel plan.

B Complete the dialogues in the simple past tense by using the information in the dialogues.

Example **A:** We played basketball yesterday.

B: Where _did you play_ ?

A: We __played__ in the park.

1. **A:** What _____ for dessert?

    B: I ate frozen yogurt.

    A: How _____?

    B: It tasted great.

2. **A:** Did you call me yesterday?

    B: Yes, I did.

    A: What time _____?

    B: I _____ you at 10.

3. **A:** How much _____ for the jacket?

    B: I paid 600 dollars for it.

    A: Where _____?

    B: I bought it at Daisy's.

4. **A:** Where _____ with your girlfriend yesterday?

    B: We went to the movies yesterday.

    A: What movie _____?

    B: We watched a horror movie.

5. **A:** How was your holiday?

    B: It was relaxing.

    A: What _____?

    B: I just stayed home and baked.

    A: What _____?

    B: I baked some cookies and bread.

C Complete the wh- questions in the simple past tense by using the information in the answers.

Example   Q: ___Where did she go___ ?
A: She went to the bank.

1. Q: _____ color suits _____?
   A: They wore black suits.

2. Q: _____ you for your birthday?
   A: He bought me a necklace for my birthday.

3. Q: _____?
   A: She cried because she saw a sad movie.

4. Q: _____?
   A: The delivery arrived three days ago.

5. Q: _____ your mom?
   A: I picked up my mom at the express bus terminal.

6. Q: _____ here?
   A: I got here by bus.

7-4. mp3

Let's Speak!

Activity-1

A Listen to the recording and check (√) the correct boxes. 🎧

Did Gina...	Yes, she did.	No, she didn't.
1. work last Saturday?	☐	☐
2. play tennis after work?	☐	☐
3. watch a movie on Sunday?	☐	☐
4. go to bed late on Sunday?	☐	☐
5. get up early on Monday?	☐	☐

B Check (√) the answers that are true for you. Then, with your partner, take turns asking and answering the questions and check your partner's answers.

Did you...	You		Your Partner	
	Yes, I did	No, I didn't	Yes, I did	No, I didn't
1. go to sleep late last night?	☐	☐	☐	☐
2. watch a movie last weekend?	☐	☐	☐	☐
3. clean your house last weekend?	☐	☐	☐	☐
4. cook dinner yesterday?	☐	☐	☐	☐
5. get up early this morning?	☐	☐	☐	☐

Activity-2

A With a partner, practice speaking by asking and answering questions about each picture. Use the simple past tense and the words given.

Example

Diana / go to the bank

A: Did Diana go to the bank yesterday?

B: No, she didn't. She went to the flower shop.

1.

Brian / work until late

2.

you and your friends /
play basketball

3.

you / find your watch

4.

they / go swimming

5.

Julia / do the laundry

6.

Edward / skip his class

Activity-3

A With a partner, practice speaking by taking turns asking and answering the following questions. Use the simple past tense and make sure to use complete sentences.

Example **A** : What time did you get up this morning?
B : I got up at 6 this morning.

1. what time / have breakfast this morning?

2. who / meet yesterday?

3. when / visit another country?

4. how much / pay for your shoes?

5. where / go for your vacation?

6. why / wear those shoes today?

7. what time / have dinner last night?

8. what / do last weekend?

9. when / graduate from high school?

10. how / get here today?

UNIT 08

Past Progressive
과거진행시제

Get Started 🎧

8-1. mp3

Read and listen to the dialogue.

Susan: Reese. I heard about what happened yesterday. Are you OK?

Reese: I'm OK. **I was having** lunch with Kelly at Apple Tree Restaurant **when** the fire alarm suddenly **went off.**

Susan: **Were people running** outside?

Reese: Yeah, so we got out of the building quickly.

Susan: I'm glad that you are safe.

Reese: Thanks. It was a bit scary.

Focus

▎과거진행시제 (Past Progressive Tense)

● 과거진행시제는 과거의 어떤 시점에 어떤 행동이 실행되거나 상황이 진행 중이었음을 말할 때 사용되며, '~을 하고 있던 중이었다'라는 의미를 나타냅니다. 과거진행시제의 문장에서 동사는 과거 진행형이 되어야 하며, 과 거진행형은 현재 진행형 [is/are + -ing] 형태에서 be 동사만 과거형으로 바꾼 [was/were + -ing] 형태입니다.

1 과거진행시제의 긍정문 (Affirmative Statements)

● 과거진행시제 문장은 구체적인 시간 표현 혹은 시간을 나타내는 시간부사절과 함께 쓰입니다.

Subject	Be Verb	Verb -ing	Time expressions
I / He / She	**was**	studying in the library	• when + past form **when** the fire alarm **went off**.
We / You / They	**were**	cleaning the floor	• while + past progressive form **while** she **was cleaning** the dishes.
It	**was**	snowing	**at** noon.

❯ 위의 예문에서 어떤 동작이 먼저 시작되었는지 알아 봅시다.

She was studying in the library **when** the fire alarm went off.
　　　　　　　　①　　　　　　　　　　　　②

We were cleaning the floor **while** she was cleaning dishes.
동시에 일어난 상황

2 과거진행시제의 부정문 (Negative Statements)

Subject	Be Verb + not	Verb -ing	Time expressions
I / He / She	**was not** (**wasn't**)	studying in the library	• when + past form **when** the fire alarm **went off**.
We / You / They	**were not** (**weren't**)	cleaning the floor	• while + past progressive form **while** she **was cleaning** the dishes.
It	**was not** (**wasn't**)	snowing	**at** noon.

❯ 축약형: I / He / She / It **was not** = I / He / She / It **wasn't**.
　　We / You / They **were not** = We / You / They **weren't**.

Exercise

A Use the words from the box to describe what was happening in each picture yesterday.

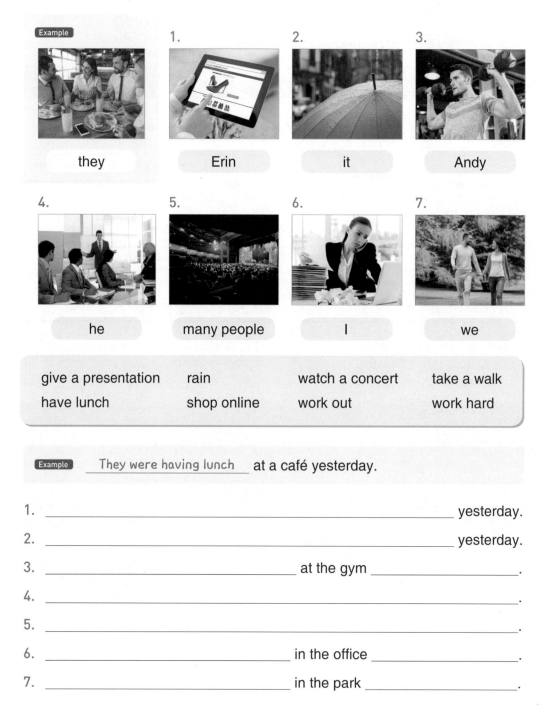

give a presentation   rain   watch a concert   take a walk
have lunch   shop online   work out   work hard

Example   _They were having lunch_ at a café yesterday.

1. _____ yesterday.
2. _____ yesterday.
3. _____ at the gym _____.
4. _____.
5. _____.
6. _____ in the office _____.
7. _____ in the park _____.

B Change the affirmative statements into negative statements.

> Example   She was brushing her teeth at 7:30 am.
>
> ➡   *She wasn't brushing her teeth at 7:30 am.*

1. Carrie and Sean were having coffee together at 4 pm.

   ➡ _____

2. Freddie and I were hiking the mountain when my phone rang.

   ➡ _____

3. Steve was reading a newspaper when he heard a siren.

   ➡ _____

4. We were waiting in line when we saw a pickpocket.

   ➡ _____

5. They were having a discussion at that time.

   ➡ _____

6. He was working on the computer when he heard a strange sound.

   ➡ _____

7. I was doing the dishes while my husband was cleaning the floor.

   ➡ _____

8. My roommate was listening to music while I was cooking dinner.

   ➡ _____

C Fill in the blanks with the correct past progressive or simple past forms of the verbs given.

> Example   Janie (watch TV) _was watching TV_ when Mark (call) _called_ her.
>
> Janice (do the laundry) _was doing the laundry_ while her husband
> (vacuum the floor) _was vacuuming the floor_.

1. Lonnie (jog) _____ when it (begin) _____ to rain.

2. Noel (do) _____ the laundry when the phone (ring) _____.

3. Alex (deliver) _____ a package when the dog (bark) _____ at him.

4. Dean (gamble) _____ while Gennie (travel) _____ around Las Vegas.

5. Rori (walk) _____ down the stairway when the power (go) _____ out.

D **Complete the passage with the past progressive forms of the verbs given.**

I am a reporter at Star Broadcasting Station. Yesterday, things didn't go well. Some reporters (move) _____ around the office quickly with reports in their hands. Some others (work on) _____ the news. I (look for) _____ some information in the Internet when my manager called me. He (look at) _____ my report when I got into his office. His assistant came in with coffee while he (shout at) _____ me. Then suddenly she tripped and spilled the coffee all over my report.

Get Started 🎧

8-2. mp3

Read and listen to the dialogue.

Wife： I just called you, but you didn't pick up the phone. **What were you doing when I called you?**

Husband： **I was talking** to my manager. What's up?

Wife： **Were you watering** the garden **while I was cooking** this morning?

Husband： **Yes, I was.**

Wife： **Was our cat playing** in the garden?

Husband： I don't think so. **Wasn't she sleeping** under the dining table?

Wife： No, she wasn't. I wonder where she went. I hope she's not missing.

Husband： Don't worry. I'm sure she's somewhere around here.

Focus

과거시제의 Yes / No 의문문 (Yes/No Questions and Short Answers)

● [Was/Were + 주어 + 동사 –ing …?]의 형태로 만듭니다.

Yes / No Questions			Short Answers	
Be Verb	Subject	Verb-ing	Affirmative	Negative
Was	I / he / she	**studying** in the library when the fire alarm went off?	Yes, you were. Yes, he / she was.	No, you were not (weren't). No, he / she was not (wasn't).
	it	**snowing** at that time?	Yes, it was.	No, it was not (wasn't).
Were	you	**sleeping** when he came in?	Yes, I was.	No, I was not (wasn't).
	we / they	**cleaning** the floor while she was cleaning the dishes?	Yes, we / they were.	No, we / they were not (weren't).

▌ 과거시제의 Wh- 의문문 (Wh- Questions and Short Answers)

● [Wh- 의문사 + was / were + 주어 + 동사 –ing …?]의 형태로 만듭니다.

Wh- word	Be Verb	Subject	Verb -ing	Answers
What	was	I	doing?	You were sleeping on the couch.
Who	were	you	talking to?	I was talking to my mom.
Where	was	he / she	going?	He / She was going home.
When	were	we / you	talking about Amy?	We / You were talking about Amy yesterday.
Why	were	you	looking at me?	I was looking at you because you changed your hairstyle.
How	were	they	doing at the new school?	They were doing fine at the new school.

Exercise

A Change the sentences into yes / no questions. Then, write short answers.

> **Example** I wasn't reading in the park this morning.
>
> ➡ **Q**: <u>Were you reading in the park this morning?</u> **A**: <u>No, I wasn't.</u>

1. Sam and David were talking loudly when the teacher came in.

   ➡ Q: _____ A: _____

   _____?

2. Ryan wasn't sleeping at midnight last night.

   ➡ Q: _____ A: _____

   _____?

3. She was studying abroad when her nephew was born.

   ➡ Q: _____ A: _____

   _____?

4. We were having a weekly meeting when the phone rang.

   ➡ Q: _____ A: _____

   _____?

5. I wasn't paying attention during the class.

   ➡ Q: _____ A: _____

   _____?

6. They were shopping while we were playing basketball.

   ➡ Q: _____ A: _____

   _____?

7. He was working at the office when a burglar broke in.

   ➡ Q: _____ A: _____

   _____?

B Use the words given to complete the questions in the past progressive
tense. Then, complete the answers and match them with the questions.

Questions	Answers

1. What (you / do) ___were you doing___ •
   at 5 yesterday?

   • a. Yes, it was.

2. (it / snow) _____ •
   last night?

   • b. Yes, they _____.

3. (Cindy / read) _____ •
   when you came in?

   • c. Because he was late for
   class.

4. Why (Mark / run) _____ •
   _____ while you were
   walking?

   • d. I (work) _____.

5. (Peter and Dan / sleep) _____ •
   _____
   in class this morning?

   • e. No, he _____.

6. What (you / hide) _____ •
   _____ when I came in?

   • f. No, she _____.

7. (he / talk on the phone) _____ •
   _____
   in the hallway?

   • g. Nothing. I wasn't hiding
   anything from you.

c Use the words given to make questions in the past progressive tense. Then, use the words given to answer them in complete sentences.

Example   who / they / meet / at 6:30   their professor

➡ Who were they meeting at 6:30?   They were meeting their professor.

1. where / you / wait for me / yesterday   in the library

    ➡ _____   _____

    _____ ?   _____

2. what / he / do / during the class   talk on the phone

    ➡ _____   _____

    _____ ?   _____

3. who / you / call / when / I / enter / the room   a repairman

    ➡ _____   _____

    _____ ?   _____

4. what / Tom / buy / when / the policeman / come   a pack of cigarettes

    ➡ _____   _____

    _____ ?   _____

5. why / she / run / while / he / walk   late for class

    ➡ _____   _____

    _____ ?   _____

6. where / they / go / when / we / see / them   to the supermarket

    ➡ _____   _____

    _____ ?   _____

Let's Speak!

Activity-1

A With a partner, practice speaking by asking and answering questions about what the people in each picture were doing at 9 pm yesterday. Use the past progressive tense and the words given. Then, ask your partner what he / she was doing at that time yesterday.

Sarah

drink with friends

John

brush his teeth

Helen

study in the library

9 pm yesterday

Lily

talk on the phone

Peter

play online games

Tyler

watch TV

> **Example** **A :** What was John doing at 9 pm yesterday?
> **B :** He was brushing his teeth.

B With a partner, look at the picture and practice speaking by asking and answering questions about what each student was doing when the professor came into the classroom. Use the past progressive tense and the words from the box.

sleep	look out the window	listen to music
drink soda	work on the laptop	play a game

Example   **A :** What was Tanya doing when the professor came in?

B : She was listening to music.

Activity-2

A With a partner, look at the picture and practice speaking by asking and answering questions about what the people were doing at 2 pm yesterday. Use the past progressive tense and the words from the box.

play the piano	practice golf
play a video game	vacuum the floor

Example A: What was David doing at 2 pm yesterday?
B: He was practicing golf.

Activity-3

A Listen to the recording and check (✓) the correct boxes. Then with a partner, practice speaking by asking and answering questions about the information. 🎧

	What a Shame!!!!	Yes	No
Alex	1. Was Alex cleaning the hallway?	☐	☐
	2. Were people laughing at him when they saw him?	☐	☐
	3. Was he pulling along toilet paper from the back of his pants?	☐	☐

Example   **A**: Was Alex cleaning the hallway?

B: No, he wasn't. He was coming out of the bathroom.

UNIT 09

Questions
의문문

PART **1**   Who told you that?

Get Started

9-1. mp3

Read and listen to the dialogue.

Ashley: Did you know that Susie and Mark are going out?

David: No way! They are like enemies.

Ashley: I know. Isn't that surprising?

David: Anyway, **who told you that? Who saw them together?**

Ashley: Leslie. She saw them in the movie theater. She said they were holding hands.

David: Well, I hope they stay together for a long time.

Ashley: I hope so, too.

Focus

▌Wh– 주어 의문문 (Wh- Questions: asking about the subject)

● 의문사가 주어인 의문문으로 [의문사 + 동사 …?]의 어순으로 만들어집니다. '누가(who) 혹은 무엇이(what) ~ 합니까/입니까?'의 뜻으로 문장의 주어에 대해 물을 때 사용됩니다. 다시 말하면, 의문사가 바로 문장의 주어 이기 때문에 [주어 + 동사 …]로 평서문의 어순과 같은 형태를 띕니다.

1 현재시제(Present Tense)일 때

Be Verb	Regular Verb
Someone is at the meeting. ↓ 주어 Q: **Who** is at the meeting? 　(Who are at the meeting?(✖) A: **John and Rick are at the meeting.**	Someone knows Eric's phone number. ↓ 주어 Q: **Who** knows Eric's phone number? A: **Victor knows Eric's phone number.**
Something is in the box. ↓ 주어 Q: **What** is in the box? 　(What are in the box? (✖) A: **Balls are in the box.**	Something makes people happy. ↓ 주어 Q: **What** makes people happy? A: **Surprise parties make people happy.**

> 현재시제 의문사 주어 의문문에서 주어는 항상 단수 취급하므로, 동사도 항상 단수형이어야 합니다.

2 과거시제 (Past Tense)일 때

Be Verb	Regular Verb
Someone was late for work. ↓ 주어 Q: **Who** was late for work? 　(Who were late for work? (✖) A: **Shaun and Ken were late for work.**	Someone saw the movie. ↓ 주어 Q: **Who** saw the movie? A: **Shirley saw the movie.**
Something was on the table. ↓ 주어 Q: **What** was on the table? 　(What were on the table? (✖) A: **Plates were on the table.**	Something happened to Susan. ↓ 주어 Q: **What** happened to Susan? A: **She lost her ring.**

> 과거시제 의문사 주어 의문문에서 주어는 항상 단수 취급하므로, 동사도 항상 단수형이어야 합니다.

Exercise

(A) **Match the questions with the correct answers and write the correct answer letters in the blanks.**

Questions	Answers
_____ 1. Who lives there?	a. The school band recorded it.
_____ 2. What's flying over your head?	b. A headache is bothering me.
_____ 3. What happened?	c. A bird is flying over my head.
_____ 4. Who recorded that song?	d. My car broke down.
_____ 5. What is bothering you?	e. Mike and Andy were there.
_____ 6. Who knows Kelly's phone number?	f. My dog makes me happy.
_____ 7. Who teaches that class?	g. Professor Norris teaches that class.
_____ 8. Who wants more coffee?	h. Wendy knows her number.
_____ 9. What makes you happy?	i. Mr. and Mrs. Lee live there.
_____ 10. Who was in the office at 10 pm?	j. Cathy and I want more.

B Change the sentences into questions about the subjects. Then, write your own answers.

> Example Someone dropped the wallet.

> → **Q**: _Who dropped the wallet?_ **A**: _Susan dropped it._

1. Someone likes horror movies.

   → Q: _____? A: _____

2. Someone speaks French well.

   → Q: _____? A: _____

3. Someone wore pink pants to work.

   → Q: _____? A: _____

4. Someone is behind the door.

   → Q: _____? A: _____

5. Someone was angry at Carol.

   → Q: _____? A: _____

6. Something makes Thomas busy.

   → Q: _____? A: _____

7. Something is burning in the kitchen.

   → Q: _____? A: _____

8. Someone gave Erin some chocolates.

   → Q: _____? A: _____

9. Someone helped the homeless.

   → Q: _____? A: _____

10. Something made her upset.

   → Q: _____? A: _____

11. Something was on the couch.

   → Q: _____? A: _____

Get Started

9-2. mp3

Read and listen to the dialogue.

Amy： You like your new place, **don't you**?

Brian： I do, but it's too far from work.

Amy： Really? You live in Longwood, **don't you**?

Brian： Yes, I do.

Amy： That's not that bad. There is plenty of public transportation in Longwood, **isn't there**?

Brian： That's true. But the buses and subway are always full of people.

Amy： Then, why don't you drive to work? You have a car, **don't you**?

Brian： Yeah, but the traffic is really bad.

Focus

▌ 부가 의문문 (Tag Questions)

- 부가 의문문은 자신이 한 말에 대해 상대방의 동의를 구할 때, 평서문의 끝에 덧붙이는 의문문을 말합니다.

1 부가 의문문 만드는 방법

① 평서문이 긍정이면, 부가 의문문은 부정형을 사용합니다.

평서문(긍정), 부가 의문문(부정)?

Be verb	평서문의 동사가 Be 동사면, 부가 의문문에서도 Be 동사를 사용합니다.	
	현재시제	He <u>is</u> tall, **isn't he**? I <u>am</u> next, **aren't I**? NOTE 평서문의 주어가 I인 경우, aren't I를 사용
	과거시제	I <u>was</u> nice to him, **wasn't I**? They <u>were</u> in Europe, **weren't they**?
Regular Verbs	평서문의 동사가 일반동사일 경우, 부가 의문문에서는 일반동사의 의문문을 만들 때처럼 조동사 do / does / did를 사용합니다.	
	현재시제	Tom <u>lives</u> downtown, **doesn't he**? NOTE 부가 의문문에서는 반드시 대명사 사용 (*doesn't Tom? (X))
	과거시제	You <u>took</u> the bus yesterday, **didn't you**?

② 평서문이 부정이면, 부가 의문문은 긍정형을 사용합니다.

평서문(부정), 부가 의문문(긍정)?

Be verb	현재시제	He isn't tall, **is he**?
	과거시제	I wasn't late, **was I**? They weren't in Europe, **were they**?
Regular Verbs	현재시제	Tom doesn't live downtown, **does he**?
	과거시제	You didn't take the bus yesterday, **did you**?

2 부가 의문문에 대한 답

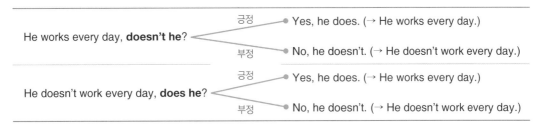

He works every day, **doesn't he**?
　긍정 ● Yes, he does. (→ He works every day.)
　부정 ● No, he doesn't. (→ He doesn't work every day.)

He doesn't work every day, **does he**?
　긍정 ● Yes, he does. (→ He works every day.)
　부정 ● No, he doesn't. (→ He doesn't work every day.)

3 부가 의문문의 억양

● 부가 의문문은 주로 대화체에서 많이 사용되며, 끝을 올리고 내리는 억양에 따라 같은 부가 의문문이 다른 뜻을 전달할 수 있습니다.

불확실한 정보를 물어볼 때: 상승 억양	Leena is not angry, **is she**? → 화자는 리나가 화가 났는지 아닌지 확실히 모르는 상태여서, 이를 알고 싶어함
상대의 재확인 또는 동의를 구할 때: 하강 억양	Leena is not angry, **is she**? → 화자는 리나가 화가 난 것이 아닐 거라 추측하지만, 상대에게 이를 확인하고 싶어함 Leena gets angry easily, **doesn't she**? → 화자는 리나에 대해 언급하고 이에 대해 상대에게 동의를 구하고 있음

Exercise

A Match the statements with the correct tag questions.

1. Professor Wilson was very angry,   •

2. Susan didn't buy the painting,   •

3. They live on Fifth Avenue,   •

4. Rick got a new job,   •

5. He doesn't drive to work,   •

6. Jasmin wants sandwiches for lunch, •

7. That isn't a good idea,   •

8. I am a hard worker,   •

9. There was a strange person in the •
   alley,

• a. didn't he?

• b. doesn't she?

• c. wasn't he?

• d. aren't I?

• e. don't they?

• f. wasn't there?

• g. does he?

• h. is it?

• i. did she?

B Look at the pictures and write the correct tag questions. Then, write short answers.

17:00

Example

Q: They arrived at 5 o'clock at the airport, _didn't they_ ?
A: _Yes, they did_ .

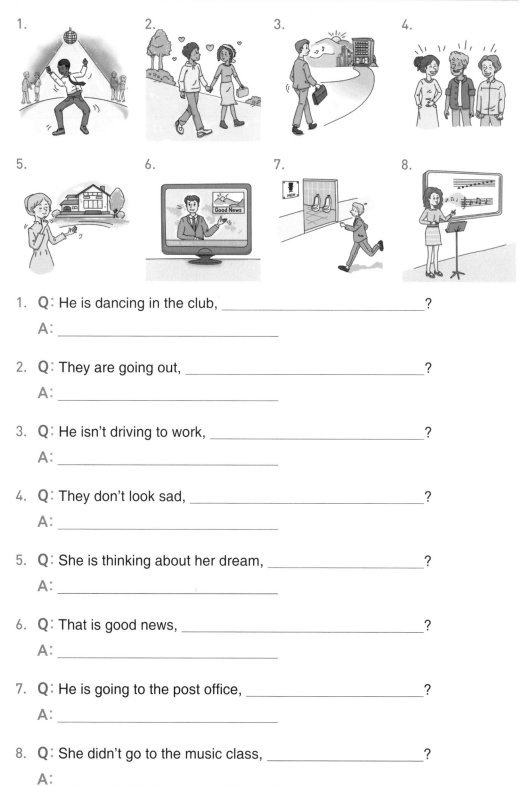

1. **Q:** He is dancing in the club, _____?

   A: _____

2. **Q:** They are going out, _____?

   A: _____

3. **Q:** He isn't driving to work, _____?

   A: _____

4. **Q:** They don't look sad, _____?

   A: _____

5. **Q:** She is thinking about her dream, _____?

   A: _____

6. **Q:** That is good news, _____?

   A: _____

7. **Q:** He is going to the post office, _____?

   A: _____

8. **Q:** She didn't go to the music class, _____?

   A: _____

Let's Speak!

Activity-1

Student A

A Ask your partner (Student B) questions about the subjects of the sentences and fill in the blanks in the sentences with your partner's answers. At the end, compare your sentences with your partner's.

> Example _____ took her to the party.
>
> **Student A** : Who took her to the party?
> **Student B** : Her sister took her to the party.
>
> → _Her sister_ took her to the party.

1. _____ asked questions about the math exam.

2. _____ sold his car and bought a new one.

3. _____ hit a bike yesterday.

4. _____ likes animals.

5. _____ are in Egypt.

B Answer your partner's questions by reading the following sentences.

> Example **A dress** is in the box.

1. **Tom** was late today.

2. **The manager** paid for the dinner.

3. **Ms. Wilson** wrote a long letter to Susan.

4. **Classical music** makes me happy.

5. **The flowers** smell good in that room.

Student B

(A) Answer your partner's questions by reading the following sentences.

> **Example**   **Her sister** took her to the party.

1. **Wendy** asked questions about the math exam.

2. **Rick** sold his car and bought a new one.

3. **A truck** hit a bike yesterday.

4. **Sarah** likes animals.

5. **Pyramids** are in Egypt.

(B) Ask your partner (Student A) questions about the subjects of the sentences and fill in the blanks in the sentences with your partner's answers. At the end, compare your sentences with your partners.

> **Example**   _____ is in the box.
>
> Student B : What is in the box?
>
> Student A : A dress is in the box.
>
> →   _A dress_   is in the box.

1. _____ was late today.

2. _____ paid for the dinner.

3. _____ wrote a long letter to Susan.

4. _____ makes me happy.

5. _____ smell good in that room.

Activity-2

(A) Listen to the recordings and check whether the intonation of each tag question rises or falls. 🎧

		Rising Intonation	Falling Intonation
1	A: Ray didn't finish his final paper, did he? B: Yes, he did. He finished it already.	☐	☐
2	A: Today's presentation was very successful, wasn't it? B: Definitely, yes.	☐	☐
3	A: The manager canceled the meeting, didn't she? B: We are not sure yet.	☐	☐
4	A: That guy looks handsome, doesn't he? B: Hmm... I don't really agree with you.	☐	☐
5	A: Jade and Joy aren't twins, are they? B: Yes, they are.	☐	☐
6	A: I was just in time, wasn't I? B: Yes, you were.	☐	☐

UNIT 10

Modal Verbs

조동사

PART 1 I can speak Spanish.

Get Started

10-1. mp3

Read and listen to the dialogue.

Bob: **Can** you speak Spanish, Jen?

Jen: Yes, I **can**. Why do you ask?

Bob: Hmm. **Can** you help me translate these documents into Spanish? There are about ten pages.

Jen: But I have a lot of other work to do.

Bob: I **can** pay you money. I **can't** translate them all by myself.

Jen: OK. I'll see if I **can** make some time in the afternoon.

Bob: Thank you so much!

Focus

▌**조동사** (Modal Verbs): **can, could, will, would, should**

- 조동사는 단독으로 쓰이지 못하며, 항상 본동사의 앞에 위치하여 본동사의 고유한 뜻에 능력, 요구, 부탁, 의무, 제안 등의 의미를 덧붙여 주는 기능을 합니다.

  I dance 춤을 추다 ― I can dance. 춤을 출 수 있다. [능력]

- 조동사 다음에는 반드시 동사원형이 옵니다.

  He dances. (○) ▌He can dances. (×) ▌He can dance. (○)

- 주어의 인칭과 수에 따라 형태가 달라지지 않습니다.

  He cans drive. (×) ▌He can drive. (○)

▌능력(Ability)의 의미를 나타내는 조동사: Can / Could

1. Can + 동사원형

● '~할 수 있다'는 뜻으로 현재 어떤 것을 할 수 있는 능력이나 어떤 것이 가능함을 나타냅니다. 부정형은 cannot 또는 can't 입니다.

긍정문	I **can** cook Italian food.
부정문	Julia **can't** speak French, but she **can** read it.
의문문	**Can** you play tennis? - Yes, I **can**. I - No, I **cannot**. (=**can't**)

2. Could + 동사원형

● '~할 수 있었다'는 뜻으로, 과거에 어떤 것을 할 수 있는 능력이나 어떤 것이 가능하였음을 나타냅니다. 부정형은 could not 또는 couldn't 입니다.

긍정문	I **could** read and write some Chinese letters when I was seven years old.
부정문	He **could not**/ **couldn't** drive a car last year.
의문문	**Could** she play the piano when she was young? - Yes, she **could**. I No, she **couldn't**.

Exercise

A Fill in the blanks by using *can't/couldn't* with the correct verbs from the box.

> sing   go   watch   find   pass   hear   drive   swim

Example I am tone-deaf, so I _can't sing_ very well.

1. I _____ what you're saying because the music is too loud.

2. Tom _____ the test because he didn't study hard.

3. Jane won't go in the water because she _____.

4. Where are my keys? I _____ them anywhere.

5. I _____ the movie until the end because it was too scary.

6. Elliot _____ to work today because he is sick.

7. David _____ a year ago, but now he is the best driver.

B Look at the pictures and make questions and answers by using *can / can't* with the words from the box.

open the jar	fly an airplane	ride the roller coaster
ride a bicycle	use a computer	ski well

Example

1.

2.

4.

5.

6.

Example **Q** : _____Can_____ he _ride the roller coaster_ ? **A** : _No, he can't._

1. **Q** : _____ she _____ ? A : _____

2. **Q** : _____ he _____ ? A : _____

3. **Q** : _____ she _____ ? A : _____

4. **Q** : _____ he _____ ? A : _____

5. **Q** : _____ she _____ ? A : _____

PART 2 Can you help me for a moment?

Get Started

10-2. mp3

Read and listen to the dialogue.

Ron: You look so stressed out. What are you working on?

Nicole: I'm preparing for my presentation tomorrow. **Can** you help me for a moment?

Ron: Sure. How **can** I help you?

Nicole: Hmm... **Will** you proofread this information?

Ron: Sure. That's not hard.

Nicole: There's more, actually. **Could** you also make some slides for me?

Ron: Sorry, I **can't**. I don't have time to do that.

Focus

요구, 부탁(request)의 의미를 나타내는 조동사: Will / Can / Would / Could

- [Will / Can / Would / Could + 주어 + 동사원형 + …?] 구조의 의문문이 상대방에게 어떤 일을 해 달라고 요구하거나 부탁할 때 '~해 주시겠습니까?'라는 의미를 전달하기 위해서 사용됩니다.

Request	Peter, **will / can / would / could** you hold my files for a second? **Will / Can / Would / Could** you open the window, (please)?
Accepting (요구 수용)	Sure, **I can / will.** | Of course. | Certainly.
Refusing (요구 거절)	No, **I can't / won't.** | Sorry, my hands are full too. NOTE 거절 시에는 거절 이유도 덧붙여 말하는 것이 좋습니다.

> can / will / could / would는 서로를 대신해서 사용될 수 있지만, 보다 예의를 갖추어 부탁할 경우에는 could / would를 사용합니다.

Exercise

A Complete the questions by using the words given in the parentheses with the words from the box.

answer my phone	show me your notes	clean up your room
stop by	be quiet	turn on the fan
hold these files	carry the box	shut the door

Example (Can you~?)

A: Lily, _can you turn on the fan_ ? it's hot in this room.

B: Sure.

1. (Can you~?)

A: _____, Tom? I can't concentrate.

B: Sorry.

2. (Will you~?)

A: _____, please? It's noisy outside.

B: Sure, I will.

3. (Would you~?)

A: Wendy, _____? I was absent yesterday.

B: I'm sorry. I was absent, too.

4. (Can you~?)

A: _____ for me? My hands are full.

B: OK. Where should I take it?

5. (Will you~?)

    A: I'm going to the meeting. _____?

    B: Sure. I'll take any messages for you.

6. (Can you~?)

    A: Ron, _____? It's so messy in here.

    B: OK, mom.

7. (Would you~?)

    A: _____ on your way home?

    B: Today? Sorry, I'm going to the airport right after work.

8. (Could you~)

    A: _____ for a second, please? I need
        to tie my shoelaces.

    B: Of course.

Get Started

10-3. mp3

Read and listen to the dialogue.

Ian: My eye is swollen again.

Amber: Let me see. Has it happened before?

Ian: Yeah, it's happened a few times before.

Amber: You **should** see an eye doctor.

Ian: Do you think I **have to** see a doctor? It doesn't hurt.

Amber: But it might be an infection. You **must** see a doctor before it gets worse.

Ian: OK, then. I'll go see an eye doctor after work.

Focus

▌의무(Obligation)의 의미를 나타내는 조동사: should / have to / must

● '~해야만 한다'는 의미를 나타냅니다.

1 Should

● 상대에게 '~하기'를 제안하거나 충고할 때 사용됩니다.

Rick has sore eyes. He **should** see an eye doctor.

Erin is very tired. Erin **should not / shouldn't** drive.

Should we all attend the meeting? – Yes, you **should**. ▌ – No, you **shouldn't**.

2 Have to

● 상대에게 어떤 행동에 대한 의무나 필요성을 언급할 때 사용됩니다.

① Have to는 should, must와는 달리 [had(have의 과거형) to + 동사원형]의 형태로 과거형이 존재하여 과거의 의무나 필요를 나타낼 수 있습니다.

과거	I **had to** clean my house last night.
현재	I **have to** clean my house today.

② Have to는 주어가 3인칭 단수인 경우 has to를 사용하는 것에 주의해야 합니다.

I / You / They / We **have to** finish the paper by today.

He / She / It **has to** go back home.

③ Have to는 다른 조동사와는 달리 부정문 / 의문문을 만들 때 조동사 do를 필요로 합니다.

부정문	**I don't have to** clean the house today. He **doesn't have to** clean the house today. We **didn't have to** clean the house last night.
의문문	**Do** you **have to** go home early? - Yes, I **do.** ⏐ No, I **don't.** **Does** she **have to** go home early? - Yes, she **does.** ⏐ No, she **doesn't.** **Did** they **have to** go home early? - Yes, they **did.** ⏐ No, they **didn't.**

3 Must

● 상대에게 보다 강한 충고를 하거나 반드시 지켜야 하는 의무, 규칙, 필요 등을 알려줄 때 사용됩니다.

You **must** tell me the truth.

We **must not / mustn't** park in this area.

He **must not / mustn't** tell a lie.

> Must로 의문문을 만들 수 없습니다.
>
> Must I tell you the truth? (X)

4 Should not / do not have to / must not의 의미 차이

● 세 가지 조동사 부정형의 의미 차이를 아래 예문을 통해 구별해 보세요.

You **should not** drive over the speed limit.   제한 속도를 넘겨서 운전해서는 안 된다.

You **must not** drive over the speed limit.   제한 속도를 넘겨서 운전하지 말아야 한다.

You **don't have to** drive over the speed limit. 제한 속도를 넘겨서 운전하지 않아도 된다.

                                      (제한 속도를 넘겨서 운전할 필요가 없다.)

Exercise

A Fill in the blanks by using *should/shouldn't* with proper words from the box.

watch	take	work	apologize
go to bed	blow	get	drive	talk

Example You look so tired these days. *You shouldn't go to bed* late.

1. You _____ too fast. You are already going over the speed limit.

2. Helen _____ harder. Her supervisor is mad because she is lazy.

3. He _____ a medium size jacket. A large one is too big for him.

4. They _____ to their manager about the problem.

5. You _____ TV so close. It's bad for your eyes.

6. Rick lost Gina's book. So he _____ to her.

7. You _____ that road. There is always a terrible traffic there.

8. You _____ your nose during an official dinner.

B Use the words given to make questions that start with *should*. Then, complete the short answers.

Example (quit the job? / No) ➡ *Should I quit the job? / No, you shouldn't*

1. (buy this dress? / No)
   ➡ _____

2. (invite Greg for dinner? / Yes)
   ➡ _____

3. (go to class tomorrow? / Yes)
   ➡ _____

4. (change tires? / Yes)
   ➡ _____

5. (make a reservation? / Yes)
   ➡ _____

6. (vote for Mr. Gordon? / No)
   ➡ _____

7. (get a medical checkup? / Yes)
   ➡ _____

C Fill in the blanks by using *have to* in the present tense. Use the negative forms where needed.

Example Mary _doesn't have to_ pay Jim back. Jim doesn't want it back.

1. I _____ be ready for the party. The party is cancelled.

2. You _____ help Jason with his homework. He can finish it by himself.

3. Andy _____ go to the hospital. He needs to get a medical checkup.

4. We _____ hand in the paper today. Dr. Emerson gave us a one-week extension.

5. _____ Susie _____ sing at the ceremony? She's not feeling well.

6. _____ you _____ wear that shirt? It's dirty.

Ⓓ **Complete the questions by using the information in the answers.**

> Example   Q: _Do I have to take a Spanish course this semester?_
> A: Yes, you have to take a Spanish course this semester.

1. Q: _____?
   A: No, he doesn't have to take the driving test again.

2. Q: _____?
   A: Yes, I have to exercise every day.

3. Q: How much _____?
   A: You have to pay $20 per each book.

4. Q: How long _____?
   A: He has to stay in the training camp for a week.

5. Q: _____?
   A: Yes, you have to work this Saturday.

6. Q: _____ Jane _____?
   A: No, she doesn't have to leave before 7.

E **Fill in the blanks by using *have to* in the tenses given.**

> Example   _I had to_   go and see Professor Smith yesterday. (past)

1. My brothers and sisters all _____ clean their rooms. (present)

2. Mark _____ attend a business seminar yesterday. (past)

3. He couldn't finish his essay yesterday. He _____ finish it today. (present)

4. They want to travel around the US. They _____ get visitor visas first. (present)

5. They _____ fix their car today. They need to go on a trip tomorrow. (present)

6. Jane _____ wait for her guest for two hours at the airport yesterday. (past)

F Fill in the blanks with *don't have to / doesn't have to / mustn't*.

> **Example** You _mustn't_ make loud noise in the library.

1. He _____ speak rudely to his boss.

2. She _____ make a speech. The conference is cancelled.

3. You _____ tell anyone about this problem. It's a secret between you and me.

4. Victor _____ get up early tomorrow. It's his day off.

5. Students _____ park in this parking lot. It's for staff only.

6. Male employees _____ wear a tie in the office. It's not required.

PART 4

Would you like some water?

Get Started 🎧

Read and listen to the dialogue.

Sylvia : Wow! It is so hot today.

Gary : Yes, it is. **Would you like** some water?

Sylvia : Sure. I'm very thirsty.

Gary : By the way, are we taking the bus to the Olympic Stadium?

Sylvia : I think the traffic will be bad on Olympic Avenue. **Why don't we** take the subway?

Gary : The subway station is too far away from here. **Let's** just take the bus.

Focus

▌ 제안(Suggestion)의 의미를 나타내는 표현:

Would you like...? / Let's... / Why don't we...? / Why not...?

1 Would you like...?

● [Would you like + 명사 / to + 동사원형 …?] 형태의 의문문으로, '~을 원하십니까?' 혹은 '~을 하고 싶습니까?' 라는 의미를 나타내기 위해서 사용됩니다.

Would you like + noun?	**Would you like** some drinks? Yes, I would. ❙ Yes, please. ❙ No, thanks.
Would you like + to verb?	**Would you like to** drink something? Yes, I would (= I'd) like to. ❙ No, thanks.

2 Let's + (not) + verb

● '우리 ~하자'라고 제안할 때 쓰는 표현으로, 이와 반대로 '~하지 말자'고 할 때는 let's 와 동사 사이에 not을 넣습니다.

Let's have lunch together. ❙ **Let's not** take a bus.

3 Why don't we / Why not + verb …?

● '우리 ~하는 게 어떻습니까?'란 의미의 표현이며, [Why don't you + verb …?]는 상대방에게 '~하는 것이 어떠세요?'라고 제안할 때 사용하는 표현입니다.

Why don't we take a break?   – Sure. Let's do that.

Why not take a break?   – I can't. I don't have time.

You look very tired. **Why don't you** take a break? 매우 피곤해 보이는데, 잠깐 쉬는 게 어때요?

Exercise

(A) **Use the words given to make questions that start with *Would you like*.
Then, write your own answers.**

Example (some cookies)   Q: ___Would you like some cookies___ ?
                           A: ___No, thanks. I'm already full.___

1. (a cup of coffee)   Q: _____?
                              A: _____

2. (play tennis)   Q: _____?
                              A: _____

3. (go to the movies)   Q: _____?
                              A: _____

4. (take a break)   Q: _____?
                              A: _____

5. (a sandwich)   Q: _____?
                              A: _____

6. (a piece of cake)   Q: _____?
                              A: _____

7. (come to my birthday party) Q: _____?
                                A: _____

8. (have dinner together)   Q: _____?
                              A: _____

B Complete the next sentences by using *Let's/Let's not* with the words from the box.

turn on the light	go to Bali	take a class together
go home	hurry	turn on the heater
go clubbing	drive	go to the supermarket

Example   It's so cold in here. _Let's turn on the heater._

1. I want to go dancing. _____

2. I think we are late for class. _____

3. I'm exhausted. I can't work anymore. _____

4. I want to study Japanese. _____

5. This place is so dark. _____

6. There is nothing to eat in the refrigerator. _____

7. Summer vacation is coming soon. _____

8. I think there will be heavy traffic. _____

C Correct the errors in the sentences.

Example   Why not ~~going~~ to the year-end party today?
                              go

1. Let's waiting for one more hour.

2. Let's eat not after 7 o'clock.

3. Why not going shopping together?

4. Would you like joining us for lunch?

5. Why not we turn the volume down a little bit?

6. Why don't we having a meeting tomorrow?

D **Read the dialogues and underline the sentences that show suggestions.**

1. A: <u>Let's go clubbing tonight.</u>

   B: Sure. <u>Let's go to Lucky Star.</u>

   A: Oh, I'm so excited.

2. A: I'm exhausted. I'm out of energy.

   B: <u>Why don't we take a break?</u>

   A: Can we do that? We don't have much time to finish the project.

   B: Well... I think we can. <u>Why not take a short break?</u>

   A: OK. <u>Let's continue after a short break.</u>

3. A: Would you like to order?

   B: Let's see... Hmm... Would you recommend something?

   A: Of course. I recommend the lunch special. Today we have cream sauce pasta with shrimp.

   B: Oh, that sounds good. I'd like to have that.

   A: Sure. And would you like to order a drink?

   B: I'll just have a glass of water, please.

   A: <u>Why don't you have a glass of soda?</u> Soda is included in the lunch special.

   B: Okay, then I will have Sprite.

Let's Speak!

10-5. mp3

Activity-1

A Practice speaking by asking your classmates *can / could* questions using the information given. If they answer yes, write their names in the boxes.

Find someone who...	Name
1. can swim	
2. can run 100 meters in under 13 seconds	
3. can speak two foreign languages	
4. can make coffee	
5. can drive a car	
6. could play the piano when he / she was a child	
7. could ride a bicycle before he / she entered elementary school	
8. can dance very well	
9. can eat meat	
10. _____	

Example Julia, can you _____? Yes, I can. I No, I can't.

Activity-2

A With a partner, practice speaking by taking turns making requests and refusing politely. Use *can / could / will / would* and the information given.

Requests	Reasons for Refusing
1. drive me home	didn't bring my car
2. help me with my homework	be busy now
3. buy me a cup of coffee	have no money
4. speak up a little bit	have a sore throat
5. lend me your tablet	need it now
6. help me carry these boxes	be in a hurry
7. review this report	have an urgent meeting
8. arrange these books on the table	have to go to school now
9. watch my bag for a second while I go to the restroom	have to leave now
10. _____	_____

Example A: Can / Will / Could / Would you _____(Request)_____ ?
B: I'm sorry, but I can't. __(Reason for Refusing)__

Activity-3

A With a partner, practice speaking by asking and answering questions about the rules in the following places. Use the words given.

In a Theater

take photos	use a phone	eat food	kick the seat in front of you	talk

Example A: Can we __take photos__ in a theater?

B: __No, we can't__. __We must not take photos__ in the theater.

In a Dormitory

smoke	cook in a room	invite friends for an overnight stay	have pets	make loud noises after 9 pm

Example A: Can we __smoke__ in a dormitory?

B: __No, we can't__. __We must not smoke__ in a dormitory.

Activity-4

A Listen to the conversations and check (✓) whether the suggestions are accepted or refused. If a suggestion is refused, write down the reason. 🎧

Conversation	Accepted	Refused	Reasons
1			
2			
3			
4			

B With a partner, practice speaking by taking turns suggesting doing the following activities together on the weekend and responding to the suggestions. When you refuse a suggestion, make sure to give a reason.

go to the movies

play cards

go swimming

go hiking

play tennis

go shopping

go out for a drink

play basketball

play soccer

play badminton

Make your own plan!

Example **Suggestion**:	Would you like to go to the movies this weekend?
	Let's go to the movies this weekend.
	Why don't we go to the movies this weekend?
Response:	Yes, I would. I Sure. Let's do that. I OK.
	Sorry, but I already have plans.

UNIT 11

Simple Future Tense

미래시제

PART 1 — What will you do tonight?

Get Started

11-1. mp3

Read and listen to the dialogue.

Adam: I'm so glad it's Friday.

Monica: Me, too. **What will you do** tonight?

Adam: I **will** probably **hang out** with Mike.

Monica: **Will you guys go** to a bar?

Adam: I think so. Why don't you join us?

Monica: Hmm. **When will you guys meet?**

Adam: At 7 pm.

Monica: OK. I **will join** you guys tonight.

Focus

▌미래시제 (Simple Future Tense): will + 동사원형

- 미래시제를 나타내는 조동사 will은 뒤에 동사원형을 수반하여 '~할 것이다'라는 의미를 전달하며, 미래에 있을 상황이나 행동에 대해 예측하여 말할 때 사용될 수 있습니다. will은 주어의 인칭이나 수에 따라 그 형태가 달라지지 않습니다.

1 긍정문 / 부정문 (Affirmative Statements / Negative Statements)

Subject	will (not)	Base Verb	
I / you / they / we / he / she / it	will will not	find	a way out.

> will은 주어와 함께 축약될 수 있습니다.
>
> I / you / they / we / he / she / it will = I / you / they / we / he / she / it'll
>
> will not은 주로 won't로 축약되어 사용됩니다.
>
> I / you / they / we / he / she / it will not = I / you / they / we / he / she / it **won't**

You will become a lawyer in the future.

He'll buy those shoes.

They won't arrive until next month.

2 의문문 (Yes / No Questions and Short Answers)

● [Will+주어+동사원형…?] 순서로 의문문을 만듭니다.

Will	Subject	Base Verb	
Will	I / you / they / we / he / she / it	find	a way out?

Short Answer (Affirmative)	Short Answer (Negative)
Yes, ➡ I / you / they / we / he / she / it **will.**	**No,** ➡ I / you / they / we / he / she / it **won't.**

> 긍정의 short answer인 경우 will은 주어와 함께 'll로 축약될 수 없으며, 반드시 will로 써야 합니다.
>
> Will you buy these shoes?   - Yes, I will. (○) | - Yes, I'll. (✘)

3 Wh- 의문문 (Wh- questions and Answers)

● [Wh- 의문사+will+주어+동사원형…?] 순서로 의문문을 만듭니다.

Wh-word	will	Subject	Base Verb + …	Answers
What		I	do next?	You will take a break.
How		you	get there?	I will take the subway.
When		he / she / it	come back?	He / She / It will come back next year.
Who	will	we	meet?	You / We'll meet the CEO of the company.
Where		you	stay?	We'll stay at the dormitory.
Why		they	leave early?	Because they have to work tomorrow.
What time		you	go home?	I'll go home at 11.
How long		they	be away?	They'll be away for a few weeks.

4 미래를 나타내는 시간 표현

● 미래시제 will은 주로 다음과 같은 시간 표현과 함께 자주 사용됩니다.

tomorrow	in the (near) future	next week
tomorrow morning	in two hours	next month
tomorrow night	in three weeks	next year

He will finish the work tomorrow.
They will become very famous in the near future.

Exercise

Ⓐ **Make predictions about the future by filling in the blanks with *will* / *won't*.**

> **Example**   In 2030, people ____will____ live on Mars.

1. We _____ see any paper books in the future.

2. In the future, people _____ travel overseas in their private jets.

3. People _____ have enough water for everyday use in the future.

4. We _____ have any oil and natural gas in the far future.

5. Time travel _____ be possible by the year 3000.

6. Someday, all men _____ raise children, and all women _____ go to work.

B Use *will / won't* to make sentences about what you will say in each situation. You may use the words given. The answers can vary.

> Example　You don't know how to swim, but your friends are talking about going for a swim. What will you say? (go / learn).
>
> ➡　　I'll go and learn. / I won't go this time.

1. You got a D on your final exam. You are talking to your friend about what you will do next term. What will you say? (study hard / skip the class)

   ➡ _____

2. You were driving fast. A policeman caught you. You have to pull your car over on the side of the road. What will you say? (drive more slowly / drive fast)

   ➡ _____

3. You and your girl / boyfriend are going to get married. You are talking about promises after marriage. What will you say? (make you happy / take care of the kids together / share the housework)

   ➡ _____

4. Your friend told you a secret. He / She doesn't want you to tell anyone. What will you say to him / her? (keep the secret / tell anyone)

   ➡ _____

C Write your own answers to the questions.

> Example　Q: When will the train leave?　　A: It ___will___ leave ___at 8:20___ .

1. Q: When will she call her friend?
   A: She _____ call _____ .

2. Q: Will Tom play tennis this Friday?
   A: _____ , _____ .

3. Q: What will he do tonight?
   A: He will _____ tonight.

4. **Q**: Where will they stay?

   A: They _____ at my house.

5. **Q**: What time will you be back?

   A: I _____ be back _____.

6. **Q**: Will they visit the old palace?

   A: _____, _____.

7. **Q**: Who will give this gift to Danni?

   A: _____ will _____ it to Danni.

8. **Q**: How will they get there?

   A: They _____ take _____.

9. **Q**: Will Mr. Swanson give us a lot of work?

   A: _____, _____.

D **Complete the dialogues in the simple future tense by using the verbs given.**

1. **A**: Andrew will quit his job.

   B: That's sad. ___What___ _____ he (do) _____ then?

   A: I think he _____ (look for) _____ a better job.

2. **A**: Hi, I have an appointment with Dr. Jones today at 3 o'clock.

   B: I'm sorry, he's not here at the moment.

   A: _____ _____ he (be back) _____

   B: I'm sure he _____ (be) _____ back soon.

   A: Then, I _____ (be) _____ back in 5 minutes.

3. **A**: Wow! Did you hear the thunder?

   B: Yes, I did. It's pouring. _____ the rain (stop) _____ soon?

   A: Yes, it will. It's a rain shower. I'm sure it _____ (last) _____
   long.

   B: How do you know? Did you see the weather forecast?

   A: Yes, I did. It _____ (be) _____ sunny after the shower.

PART 2

She is going to fly to New Zealand.

Get Started 🎧

11-2. mp3

Read and listen to the passage.

Linda made plans for the winter vacation. She **is going to fly** to New Zealand and see her sister. Her sister is studying in Auckland now. Linda doesn't like winter activities. So she wants to go to New Zealand in December and do some water sports there. Linda and her sister **are going to go** windsurfing and swimming in Mission Bay. They're also **going to explore** Hauraki Gulf. They're **going to do** some whale watching there.

Focus

▌ 미래시제 (Future Tense): **be going to+동사원형**

- [will+동사원형]과 같이 [be going to+동사원형]으로도 '~할 것이다'라는 의미인 미래시제를 표현할 수 있습니다. will은 막연한 미래를 나타내는 반면, be going to는 특히 가까운 미래에 있을 법한 일을 예측하거나 이미 세운 계획이나 결정을 말할 때 자주 사용됩니다.

> ❯ be going to에서 be 동사는 주어의 인칭과 수에 따라 달라집니다.
>
> going to는 대화에서 사용될 때, 종종 'gonna'로 발음되기도 합니다.

1 긍정문 (Affirmative Statements)

Subject	be going to	Base Verb	
I	**am going to**	change	my hairstyle.
You / We / They	**are going to**	have	breakfast soon.
He / She	**is going to**	take	a dance class next month.

2 부정문 (Negative Statements)

● [be+not+going to+동사원형 …] 의 형태로 부정문을 만듭니다. 축약형에는 주어와 be 동사를 축약하는 방법
과 be 동사와 not을 축약하는 방법 두 가지가 있습니다.

Subject	Be Verb	not	going to	Base Verb	
I	am			change	my hairstyle.
You / We / They	are	not	going to	have	breakfast soon.
He / She	is			take	a dance class next month.

We're not going to have breakfast soon. [주어와 be 동사 축약]

He isn't going to take a dance class next month. [be 동사와 not 축약]

Exercise

A Match the sentences on the left with the correct future sentences on the right.

1. Dorothy is feeling sick now. •

2. Amy called David this afternoon and left a message. •

3. Rick just bought a new car. •

4. Wendy misses her grandmother. •

5. I'm exhausted now. •

6. People are waiting for the green light. •

7. Brandon's camera is broken. •

8. It's so hot in the office. •

• a. She is going to visit her grandmother next month.

• b. She is going to see a doctor.

• c. He's going to call her back.

• d. I'm going to take a break.

• e. They are going to cross the road.

• f. He is going to take it to the customer service center.

• g. He's going to go for a drive.

• h. I'm going to turn on the air-conditioner.

B **Complete the sentences by using** *be (not) going to* **with the correct verbs from the box.**

| have | explain | talk | fix | go | ask | work out | take | begin |

Example Kate and Charlie can't come to the dinner on Saturday.

They __are going to go__ to Mexico this weekend.

1. Chris's bike is broken. So he _____ it.

2. Alice is tired of working. So she _____ a vacation.

3. James and Peter want to exercise. They _____ at the gym tomorrow.

4. This work is too difficult. I _____ someone for help.

5. I'm so full right now. I _____ dessert.

6. I already told you, but I _____ it one more time.

7. The wedding ceremony _____ in a minute. Ladies and gentlemen, please be seated.

8. Robert and Andy had an argument last night. They _____ to each other for a while.

C Look at the pictures and complete the dialogues by using *be going to* and the verbs given.

1. **A:** What is the weather forecast for tomorrow?
   B: They say it (rain) _____ tomorrow.

2. **A:** What are your vacation plans for this summer?
   B: I (spend) _____ a week in Thailand.

3. **A:** What is Matthew going to do during the spring break?
   B: He (play) _____ a lot of online games.

PART 3

What are you going to do this weekend?

Get Started

11-3. mp3

Read and listen to the dialogue.

Brandon: **What are you going to do** this weekend?

Jessica: **I'm going to take** my dog to the hospital. She needs a shot.

Brandon: Oh, I see. **Are you going to take** her to the vet next to the post office?

Jessica: Yes, I am. What about you? **What are you going to do** this weekend?

Brandon: Oh, **I'm going to go** for a bike ride.

Jessica: That sounds fun.

Focus

▌ **Yes / No 의문문** (Yes / No Questions and Short Answers)

● [Be 동사+주어+going to+동사원형 …?]의 형태로 의문문을 만듭니다.

Be Verb	Subject	going to	Base Verb		Short Answers	
					Yes,	I am. you / we / they are. he / she is.
Am **Are** **Is**	I you / we / they he / she	**going to**	buy	that car?	No,	I am not. you / we / they aren't. he / she isn't.

Are you going to take the dance class next month? – Yes, I am.

Is he going to have lunch with us? – No, he isn't.

Wh- 의문문 (Wh- questions and Answers)

● [Wh- 의문사+be 동사+주어+going to+동사원형 …?]의 형태로 의문문을 만듭니다.

Wh-word	Be Verb	Subject	going to	Base Verb		Answers
How	am	I		get	to the post office?	Just take a bus.
Who	are	you		see	this Saturday?	I'm going to see Debbie this Saturday.
When	is	he / she / it		arrive	here?	He / She / It's going to arrive next month.
What		we	going to	do	for her birthday?	We / You're going to have a party.
Where	are	you		go	for lunch?	We're going to go to a Chinese restaurant.
Why		they		work	until late?	Because they have so much work.

Exercise

(A) Use the words given to make questions and complete the answers.

> **Example** (play the organ / tonight)
>
> **Q**: Is she going to play the organ tonight ?
>
> **A**: No, she isn't. She is going to play it tomorrow.

1. (have lunch with us / today)

   Q: _____?

   A: Yes, I am.

2. (move to a new place / this weekend)

   Q: _____?

   A: No, we aren't. _____.

3. (snow / tomorrow)

   Q: _____?

   A: No, it isn't. _____.

4. (make a speech / on Monday)

Q: _____?

A: Yes, he is.

5. (join a band)

Q: _____?

A: No, I'm not. _____.

B Put the words in the correct order to make questions. Then, write your own answers.

Example   he / golf / going to / is / when / play

Q: <u>When is he going to play golf</u> ?

A: <u>He's going to play golf next Saturday.</u>

1. are / this weekend / going to / you / meet / who

Q: _____?

A: _____

2. sell / they / why / are / their books / going to

Q: _____?

A: _____

3. get to / how / going to / you / are / the hospital

Q: _____?

A: _____

4. going to / together / when / dinner / are / have / we

Q: _____?

A: _____

5. is / Jane / about / what / going to / tell you

Q: _____?

A: _____

C **In each dialogue, find the number of errors given and correct the errors.**

1. (4 mistakes)

Chris: What are you go to do this weekend?

Rachael: I am going to going to the art gallery this Saturday.

Chris: Wow! Who are you go with?

Rachael: With my roommate, Erin. Do you want to join us?

Chirs: I want to, but I watch a movie with my girlfriend.

2. (6 mistakes)

Chad: When are you going to move, Jasmine?

Jasmine: Well... I'm going to moving to a studio apartment next to the YMCA. Are you help me move?

Chad: Of course. Are Peter going to help you, too?

Jasmine: No, he is. He's going take the driving test on Friday.

Chad: Then let's ask Ben for help as well.

Get Started 🎧

11-4. mp3

Read and listen to the dialogue.

Amber: Where are you going this afternoon?

Joe: I'm going to the airport.

Amber: Are you picking someone up?

Joe: Yes, my cousins **are coming**. They are going to stay here for a couple of days with me.

Amber: So what are your plans?

Joe: Well... I'm taking them to the beach tomorrow.

Amber: That's a good idea.

Focus

미래시제 (Future Tense): be+Verb-ing

- 가까운 미래의 계획에 대해 말할 때에는 현재 진행형 [be+Verb-ing] (Unit 5 참조)을 사용할 수 있습니다.

- 다음과 같은 경우에 [be+Verb-ing]를 미래에 대해 말할 때 주로 사용합니다.

1 확정된 날짜나 시간을 언급하며 미래의 계획에 대해 말할 때

We are coming back on February 5th.

What time is he leaving tomorrow? He's leaving at 10:30.

2 앞으로 일어날 일에 대해 강한 확신을 갖고 말할 때

This dog is not going anywhere. I will take care of him.

I'm not meeting him ever again.

Exercise

(A) Fill in the blanks with the *be + -ing* simple future forms of the words from the box.

go	arrive	attend	get	work	fly	meet	have

Example I ___am working___ on Saturday, so I cannot go to the picnic.

1. Julian _____ to Amsterdam next weekend.

2. Rick and Wendy _____ married tomorrow.

3. My sister-in-law is in the hospital now. She _____ a baby soon.

4. We _____ shopping for winter clothes soon.

5. _____ you _____ your friend this evening?
   Yes, I am.

6. What time _____ your brother _____ at Heathrow Airport?
   He _____ at 8:45 pm.

7. My boss and I _____ a meeting this afternoon.

B Use the words given to make questions. Then, write your own short answers.

Example   he / come / to the Halloween party?

Q: <u>Is he coming to the Halloween party</u>?   A: <u>Yes, he is.</u>

1. you / come / to my wedding?

   Q: _____?   A: _____

2. she / go / to work / this weekend?

   Q: _____?   A: _____

3. they / play baseball / on Saturday?

   Q: _____?   A: _____

4. you / work / on the weekends too?

   Q: _____?   A: _____

5. where / we / go / after lunch?

   Q: _____?   A: _____

6. when / you / leave / for your hometown?

   Q: _____?   A: _____

7. which airline / you / take to L.A.?

   Q: _____?   A: _____

8. what time / Harry / arrive / in Chicago?

   Q: _____?   A: _____

C Read the dialogues and underline the present progressive verb forms. Then, write 'P' if they show the present tense and write 'F' if they show the future tense.

1. Holly: Are you <u>working</u>(P) on the report now?

   Adam: Yes, I am.

   Holly: You must be busy. Are you working late today?

   Adam: Yes. I have to finish this report before my supervisor leaves for a business trip.

   Holly: When is he leaving?

   Adam: Tomorrow morning.

2. Steve: Natalie, where are you going?

   Natalie: Oh, I'm going to the library now.

   Steve: I'm heading that way, too. So, Natalie, what are you doing after the final exam?

   Natalie: I'm staying home because my parents are going to visit me. How about you? What are your plans after the exam?

   Steve: I'm flying to Thailand on June 25th.

   Natalie: Oh, really? When are you coming back?

   Steve: In two weeks.

Let's Speak!

Activity - 1

A Practice speaking by asking your classmates questions in the simple future tense using the information given. If they answer Yes, write their names in the blanks.

	Find someone who...	Name
Example		

> Julia, are you going to study in the library after class?

> – Yes, I am.
> – No, I'm not.

1. study in the library after class

2. go to the movies this weekend

3. get married this year

4. meet friends tonight

5. travel abroad during the holiday

6. have Korean food for dinner

7. stay home this weekend

Activity - 2

A A check (✓) if you think these predictions will happen in the future.

1.	Aliens will attack the Earth in 20 years.	Yes ☐ No ☐
2.	My dream will come true soon.	Yes ☐ No ☐
3.	Everyone will work from home in 5 years.	Yes ☐ No ☐
4.	You will win the lottery someday.	Yes ☐ No ☐
5.	Everyone will fly to the moon in the future.	Yes ☐ No ☐
6.	You will be a millionaire in 10 years.	Yes ☐ No ☐

B With a partner, practice speaking by asking and answering questions about the predictions in A. Use the simple future tense.

> Example　**A**：Will aliens attack the Earth in 20 years?
> **B**：No, they won't.

Activity-3

A Listen to the following people talking about their plans for next year, and write the names of the people under the correct pictures. 🎧

| Julie | Brian | Lily | Vincent | Elaine | Minho |

What are they going to do next year?

1.

2.

3.

4.

5.

6.

B Talk with your partner about what you are going to do next year.

Activity-4

(A) Student A

With a partner, take turns asking and answering questions about the missing information in Dana's weekly plan and fill in the blank boxes with your partner's answers. Use the *be + -ing* simple future forms.

	Thursday	Friday	Saturday	Sunday
noon	have lunch with co-workers		have lunch with a college friend	
afternoon		meet clients		go shopping
evening	work late		have dinner with a friend	

Example
A: What is Dana doing <u>on Thursday afternoon</u>?
B: She is <u>attending a conference</u>.

B Student B

With a partner, take turns asking and answering questions about the missing information in Dana's weekly plan and fill in the blank boxes with your partner's answers. Use the *be + -ing* simple future forms.

	Thursday	Friday	Saturday	Sunday
noon		go to the bank $		go to church
afternoon	attend a conference		go to the hair salon	
evening		have a business meeting		go to a concert

Example

B: What is Dana doing _on Thursday at noon_ ?

A: She is _having lunch with co-workers_ .

Activity-5

(A) Make your own weekly plan for next week. If there are no plans for some of the times, leave the boxes blank.

My Weekly Plan

	Monday	Thesday	Wednesday	Thursday
Morning				
Afternoon				
Evening				

	Friday	Saturday	Sunday	Memo
Morning				
Afternoon				
Evening				

(B) With a partner, practice speaking by taking turns asking and answering questions about each other's weekly plans for next week. Try to find the times when you and your partner are both free.

UNIT 12

Prepositions

전치사

Get Started 🎧

12-1. mp3

Read and listen to the dialogue.

Amy： When is the English exam?

David： It's **on** Wednesday.

Amy： So, it's **on** the 19th, right?

David： That's right. Did you study a lot?

Amy： Not really. I was in the hospital **for** a couple of days because I had the flu.

David： Oh, I'm sorry to hear that. I can lend you my notes.

Amy： Oh, that's so nice of you. Thanks.

David： No problem. I'll bring them to the class **in** the afternoon.

Focus

▎시간을 나타내는 전치사 (in, on, at)

in	year, month, season, part of the day, etc.	I was born **in** 1990. My birthday is **in** June. **In** winter, the roads are slippery. I usually take a nap **in** the afternoon.
on	days of the week, specific date, etc.	We can wear casual clothes **on** Friday. We are getting married **on** September 3rd. I usually get up late **on** Saturday mornings. What are you going to do **on** the weekend? Let's hang out **on** Valentine's Day.

at	exact time, time of the day, meal time, etc.	My English class begins **at** 3:00. I'll see you **at** dinner. We usually have lunch **at** noon. I'll visit my grandparents **at** Christmas. I don't have it **at** the moment.

▌ 기간을 나타내는 전치사 (in, for, until, during)

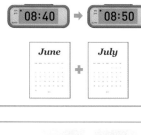

in 10 minutes
(10분 후에)

The presentation will start **in** 10 minutes.

in 2 months
(2개월 후에)

I am going to master Chinese **in** two months.

for 3 years (3년 동안)

We lived in Sydney **for** three years.

for 2 hours (2시간 동안)

I only slept **for** two hours yesterday.

until 12:15 (12시 15분까지)

The exam continued **until** 12:15.

until midnight (자정이 되도록)

They didn't get home **until** midnight.

during summer vacation
(여름 방학기간 동안)

I studied French **during** summer vacation.

during the presentation
(발표하는 동안)

Please be quiet **during** the presentation.

Exercise

(A) Put the word below under the correct prepositions.

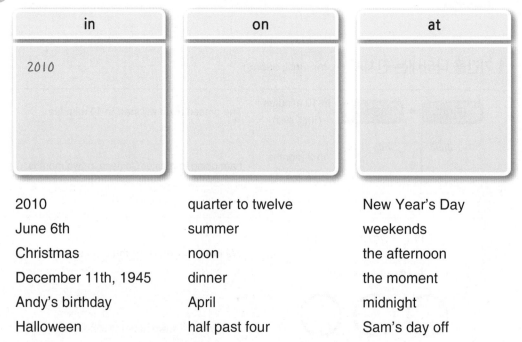

in	on	at
2010		

2010   quarter to twelve   New Year's Day

June 6th   summer   weekends

Christmas   noon   the afternoon

December 11th, 1945   dinner   the moment

Andy's birthday   April   midnight

Halloween   half past four   Sam's day off

(B) Circle the correct prepositions.

> **Example** I have a job interview (in / on / (at)) half past nine.

1. She has a biology test (in / on / at) Thursday.

2. Phil always gets up late (in / on / at) Sunday mornings.

3. We'll see you guys (in / on / at) lunch time.

4. My dad was born (in / on / at) 1969.

5. Vivian felt very nervous (in / on / at) the time.

6. (In / On / At) winter, I like to go skiing.

7. The party is (in / on / at) April 17th.

8. The presentation is (in / on / at) 3 o'clock (in / on / at) Tuesday.

C Fill in the blanks with *in / for / until / during*.

Example I went home ___during___ my lunch break.

1. I am so tired. I only slept _____ an hour last night.

2. I'll be back _____ two minutes.

3. I waited here _____ 6 o'clock.

4. Peter lived in Barcelona _____ three years.

5. Susan learned Spanish _____ her college days.

6. We'll give you a call _____ three days.

7. I can't wait _____ his return.

D Complete the dialogues by using the correct prepositions of time.

Steve： What time do you usually wake up?

Brooke： I usually wake up _____ 6 o'clock _____ the morning.

Steve： Wow! Why do you get up that early?

Brooke： Because I go to the gym _____ Monday, Wednesday, and Friday mornings.

Steve： Why do you work out so much?

Brooke： Because I have gained too much weight _____ the last year. I will lose 5kg _____ three months.

Steve： Oh, wow! Good luck! Anyway, how long do you work out at a time?

Brooke： I work out _____ an hour.

Steve： So when do you get to work?

Brooke： I get to work _____ 9.

Steve： I see. You are very diligent.

Get Started

12-2. mp3

Read and listen to the dialogue.

Paul: Excuse me, is there a bank **near** here?

Jasmine: Yes, there is one **behind** that library.

Paul: Do you mean the library **next to** the park?

Jasmine: Exactly. The bank is **behind** that library. You can't
             miss it.

Paul: Oh, thanks a lot.

Jasmine: Sure. By the way, the bank is **on** the second floor
             of the building.

Paul: Thank you so much!

Focus

▎ 위치를 나타내는 전치사 (under, next to, in front of, near, behind, between)

The ball is **under** the chair.	The ball is **next to** the chair.	The ball is **in front of** the chair.	The ball is **near** the chair.	The ball is **behind** the chair.	The ball is **between** the chair **and** the table.

장소를 나타내는 전치사 (at, on, in)

● 물건이나 사람이 어떤 특정한 지점에 위치할 때는 전치사 at, 어떤 물건이나 장소의 표면에 있을 때는 on, 어느 공간 안에 있을 때는 in을 사용합니다.

at	particular spots / places / buildings	The plane stops for an hour at Frankfurt Airport. I lost my wallet at the bus terminal. She works at the museum. Please sign at the bottom of the page. I live at the end of the street. We had a good time at the jazz concert.
on	surface of things or place	The flower shop is on the first floor. The airplane landed on the ground. We had a picnic on the grass. Someone wrote my name on the wall. The box of cereal is on the top shelf. The report card is on the table.
in	cities, countries, inside some spaces / lines	It's cold in Korea. We live in London. There are many customers in the store. We went hiking in the mountains. She keeps her jewelry in a big jar. I have a lot of Halloween candies in my pocket. Many people are standing in line.

자주 쓰이는 관용적 표현

in	in class, in the newspaper, in the hospital, in prison, in line
on	on TV, on (the) air
at	at work, at school, at church, at the movies, at the concert

Exercise

A Look at the pictures and fill in the blanks with the correct prepositions of location.

| Example | The man is standing _____in front of_____ the post office. |

1. I parked my car _____ two dump trucks.

2. He dropped his key _____ the sofa.

3. I sat _____ the space heater because I was cold.

4. The bank is _____ the supermarket.

5. The police car was right _____ my car.

6. My family took a photo _____ the Statue of Liberty.

7. Tom always wants to sit _____ Sally during meetings.

B Circle the correct prepositions.

> Example | I keep my change ((in) / on / at) my piggy bank.

1. My textbooks are (in / on / at) the desk.

2. She was (in / on / at) the basketball game yesterday.

3. He's lying (in / on / at) the floor.

4. Sally is still (in / on / at) work.

5. I usually study (in / on / at) home.

6. My uncle is (in / on / at) the airport right now.

7. My friend and I had a great time (in / on / at) the jazz concert.

8. It's windy and cold (in / on / at) Beijing.

C Fill in the blanks with the correct prepositions of place / location.

> Example | **A:** Does the bus stop __at__ the North Street station?
> **B:** Yes, it does.

1. **A:** Where is Jane?
   B: Jane is _____ home.

2. **A:** Harry speaks French well.
   B: Yes, he does. I think he was born _____ Paris.

3. **A:** Do you like painting?
   B: Yeah, I like painting graffiti _____ the wall.

4. **A:** What are you going to do _____ your birthday?
   B: I'll celebrate my birthday _____ a club.

5. **A:** Wow! So many people are standing _____ line for the women's bathroom.
   B: Let's go find another bathroom.

6. A: What did Gary tell you?

    B: He told me that the baseball game will be _____ the air at 5:00 today.

7. A: Do you know anything about Bill?

    B: He was _____ prison for three years because he robbed a bank.

8. A: Why is Fiona not answering her phone?

    B: She can't answer the phone now because she's _____ the movies.

9. A: Can you give me a hand? I can't reach the book. It's _____ the top shelf.

    B: Sure, I can help you. Is it the one _____ the right?

    A: Yes, it is. Thank you.

10. A: How come Sue is not around?

    B: She is _____ the hospital.

    A: Oh, what's wrong with her?

    B: She broke her leg while skiing.

Let's Speak!

Activity-1

A Listen to Crystal's plans for December and circle the dates you hear. Then, listen again and write down her plans for the days you circled.

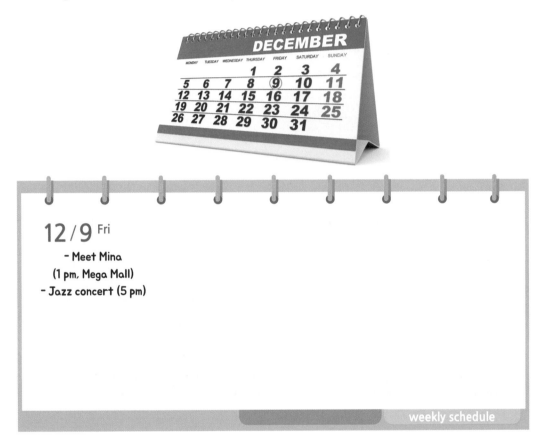

DECEMBER

MONDAY	TUESDAY	WEDNESDAY	THURSDAY	FRIDAY	SATURDAY	SUNDAY
			1	2	3	4
5	6	7	8	⑨	10	11
12	13	14	15	16	17	18
19	20	21	22	23	24	25
26	27	28	29	30	31	

12 / 9 Fri
- Meet Mina
(1 pm, Mega Mall)
- Jazz concert (5 pm)

weekly schedule

B With a partner, practice speaking by asking and answering questions about the information in A.

Example
A: When is Crystal's dad's birthday? B: It's on December 11th.
A: Where is the birthday party? B: It's at the Grand Restaurant.
A: What time does the birthday party start? B: It starts at 6 pm.

Activity-2

(A) With a partner, practice speaking by asking and answering questions about the locations of things in the picture.

Example **A:** Where is the flower bed?
         B: It's behind the bench.

(B) Draw the following things in the picture above. Then, with a partner, practice speaking by asking and answering questions about the locations of these things.

| bag | cat | girl | trash |

Activity-3

A With a partner, practice speaking by describing the locations of the people and places in the picture.

Example The convenience store is on the first floor of the building.

UNIT 13

Imperatives

명령문

PART 1   Look at this house.

Get Started 🎧

13-1. mp3

Read and listen to the dialogue.

Crystal: Hey, **look at this house**.

Andy: Wow, it looks so nice.

Crystal: Right. Well, what does the sign say on the door?

Andy: It says "**Beware of dogs**." There must be some scary dogs.

Crystal: Oh, I see them. Let's leave.

Andy: Yeah, let's get out of here.

Focus

명령문 (Imperatives)

● 명령문은 듣는 상대방에게 명령이나 주의를 줄 때 사용하는 문장입니다. 명령문의 긍정문은 주어가 없이 동사의 원형으로 시작하며, 부정문은 긍정문 앞에 Do not / Don't 를 붙입니다.

Affirmative Statements		Negative Statements		
Base Verb		**Don't**	**Base Verb**	
Sit	down.		be	upset.
Tell	me about it.	**Do not**	run	in the hallway.
Be	quiet.	**Don't**	make	loud noise.
Beware	of dogs.		touch	the animals.
			disturb.	

> 명령문의 앞 또는 뒤에 'please'를 붙이면, 예의를 갖추어 상대방에게 요청하는 의미를 나타낼 수 있습니다.
>
> **Please**, sit down. | Sit down, **please**.

Exercise

(A) Look at the picture and complete the sentences using the words from the box. When there is an ☒, make a negative sentence.

wash	watch	cry	fasten	cheat	eat
drive	clean up	be late for	open	study	get up

Example

Don't open the door.

1.

_____ the room.

2.

_____ too fast.

3.

_____ harder.

4.

_____

5.

_____

6.

_____ work.

7.

_____ your car.

8.

_____ your seatbelt.

9.

_____ food in the library.

10.

_____ your step.

11.

_____ on the test.

PART 2 Cross the road and turn left.

et Started 🎧

13-2. mp3

Read and listen to the dialogue.

Scott: Ma'am, **watch out for the car**.
Norma: Thank God! I didn't see it because I was looking at the map.
Scott: Where are you going?
Norma: Oh, I want to go to the post office, but I think I'm lost.
Scott: Just **cross the road** and **turn left**. Then you'll see the post office next to the bank.
Norma: Thank you so much.

Focus

▍ 명령문의 용법

● 명령문은 어떤 일의 순서 따위를 가르쳐주거나 길을 알려줄 때에도 사용될 수 있습니다.

	Affirmative Statements		Negative Statements		
	Base Verb		**Don't**	**Base Verb**	
Instructions	**Add**	sugar.	**Do not**	add	sugar.
	Pour	the water.	**Don't**	pour	the water.
Directions	**Turn**	left.		turn	left.
	Go	around the corner.		go	around the corner.
	Cross	the road.		cross	the road.

Exercise

A Look at the pictures and fill in the blanks with the correct verbs from the box.

> add　　pour　　grill　　chop　　bake　　microwave　　stir　　mix

1.

_____ some salt.

2.

_____ flour into a bowl.

3.

_____ the onions.

4.

_____ the potatoes.

5.

_____ the flour and butter.

6.

_____ the stew.

7.

_____ the steak.

8.

_____ the milk.

B Match the sentences with the correct pictures and write the correct answer letter in the blanks.

_____ 1. Turn left at the end of the road.

_____ 2. Go past the library.

_____ 3. Go straight for two blocks.

_____ 4. Go through the park.

_____ 5. Make a right.

_____ 6. Cross the street.

a.

b.

c.

d.

e.

f.

C Complete the dialogues by using the correct words from the box.

turn	go	walk	type	press	move	click

1. Michael: Laura, how do I download this picture?

   Laura: First, _____ the cursor to the picture. Then _____ the right mouse button and _____ 'save the picture'. _____ in the name of the picture and then save it.

   Michael: Oh, now I get it.

2. Jordan: Excuse me, I'm a freshman here. How can I get to the auditorium?

   Kimberly: _____ straight up this street for one block and _____ right. _____ past the library and go through the tennis court. Then, you'll see the auditorium. You can't miss it.

   Jordan: Wow, this campus is huge. Thanks so much.

Let's Speak!

Activity-1

A With a partner, practice speaking by taking turns making affirmative and negative imperative statements. Make at least 5 statements each for both affirmative and negative.

> **Example** **Affirmative imperative statement**: Come in, please.
> **Negative imperative statement**: Don't eat in the library.

Activity-2

A Listen to the recording and check (✓) the ingredients that are not mentioned. 🎧

cream sauce ☐	shrimp ☐	oil ☐	garlic ☐
onions ☐	spaghetti ☐	tomato sauce ☐	mushrooms ☐

B Listen to the recording again and fill in the blanks with the correct verbs from the box. Then, number the sentences in the order you hear them in the recording. 🎧

> Place   Add   Chop   Put   Boil   Put   Pour

204 Unit 13 · Imperatives

Cooking Tomato Sauce Spaghetti

☐ _____ the tomato sauce in the pan.

☐ _____ some onions and garlic.

☐ _____ spaghetti in the boiling water and boil it
for about 8 to 10 minutes.

☐ _____ the chopped onions and garlic to the sauce.

☐ _____ the tomato sauce on the spaghetti and enjoy!

☐ 1 Boil water.

☐ _____ the spaghetti on the plate.

☐ _____ the sauce over medium heat.

Activity-3

A Listen to the directions to the places in the box below. Then, write the names of the places in the correct locations in the picture. 🎧

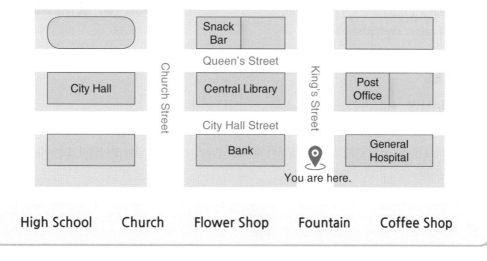

High School   Church   Flower Shop   Fountain   Coffee Shop

B With a partner, practice speaking by taking turns asking for and giving directions to the places other than the ones in the box in A.

Example **A :** How do I get to the snack bar?

B : Go straight for two blocks. Turn left at Queen's Street. It's on your right next to the coffee shop.

UNIT 14

Future Time Clauses
미래의 시간 부사절

Get Started 🎧

14-1. mp3

Read and listen to the dialogue.

Tim: What are you doing this afternoon?

Katie: I'm not really sure. The weather forecast says it will rain today.

Tim: Really? The sky is so clear now.

Katie: Yeah. Maybe the weather forecast is wrong. **If the weather is nice in the afternoon, I will go shopping.**

Tim: What if it rains?

Katie: **If it rains, I will just go home.**

Focus

조건 부사절 (Adverb Clauses – Future Conditional): If 부사절

● if로 시작하는 부사절은 미래시제 주절과 함께 사용되며, 미래에 '~이 일어난다면, ~하게 된다면'이라는 의미를 나타내는 조건절로 현재시제를 사용하여 미래를 나타냅니다. 어떤 일이 일어날지 또는 어떤 일을 하게 될지를 예측하여 말할 때 사용됩니다.

1 문장 구조

If Clause (조건): 현재시제		Main Clause (주절 – 결과): 미래시제
If + Subject + Verb (Present Tense) ~,	**+**	Subject + Verb (Future Tense) ~.
If he **gets** the job,		he **will buy** a new car.
If you **don't run**,		you **will be** late for work.
If the weather **is** nice,		we **are going to go** on a picnic.
If she **doesn't go**,		I **won't go** either.

> if절은 주절의 앞이나 뒤에 모두 올 수 있으며, 어느 위치에 있든 문장의 의미는 그대로 유지됩니다. 단, if절이 주절 앞에 오는 경우 comma(,)가 사용됩니다.
>
> **If he gets the job,** he will buy a new car. = He will buy a new car **if he gets the job.**

Exercise

A Circle the correct answers.

Example If Jeff (will buy /(buys)) me a gift, I ((will thank)/ thank) him.

1. If we (don't / won't) hurry, we (are going to be / are) late for class.

2. If it (will rain / rains / rain) tomorrow, I (won't go / don't go) hiking.

3. If we (stay / are staying) home tonight, we (watch / are going to watch) a movie.

4. We (play / will play) basketball if we (go / will go) to the park this Saturday.

5. People (will laugh / laugh) at you if you (go / are going) outside in that sweater.

6. I (wake / will wake) you up if I (got / get / will get) up early tomorrow.

7. If you (won't stop / don't stop) smoking, you (will have / have / had) health problems.

8. You (will be / are) freezing if you (won't / don't) wear a coat.

B Fill in the blanks with the correct tense forms of the verbs given.

Example If you (get) _get_ to work early, you (get) _will get_ free sandwiches.

1. If you (dream) _____ of a pig, you (win) _____ a lottery.

2. If we (take) _____ a day off tomorrow, we (go) _____ skiing.

3. If you (buy) _____ your mother a gift, she (be) _____ pleased.

4. We (go) _____ swimming if the weather (get) _____ warmer.

5. If Mark (make) _____ more money, he (buy) _____ a new sports car.

6. I (be) _____ late for class if the bus (come) _____ late.

7. If Erica (study) _____ harder, she (pass) _____ the exam.

8. I (finish) _____ the project today if everyone (help) _____ me.

What will you do after you relax?

14-2. mp3

Get Started

Read and listen to the dialogue.

Jasmine: What are you going to do when you're on vacation?

Richard: First, I'm going to get some rest.

Jasmine: Then what will you do after you relax for a while?

Richard: Maybe I'll visit my brother in L.A.

Jasmine: Sounds great. Do you have any special plans while you're there?

Richard: I'm going to travel to Death Valley.

Focus

▌ **시간 부사절** (Time Clauses – Future Time): **when, before, after, while** 등의 접속사로 시작되는 부사절

● 미래시제의 주절과 함께 사용된 when, before, after, while 등의 접속사가 이끄는 시간 부사절에서는 현재시제를 사용하여 미래의 의미를 나타냅니다.

1 문장 구조

Time Clause (시간 부사절): 현재시제		Main Clause (주절): 미래시제
When / Before / After / While / +Subject + Verb (Present Tense) ~,	**+**	Subject + Verb (Future Tense) ~.
When Mrs. Kim **comes** back,		I **will tell** her.
Before my friends **come**,		I **will clean** my room.
After I **finish** my project,		I **am going to take** a day off.
While you **are** on vacation,		I **will take** care of your dog.

> 시간 부사절은 주절의 앞이나 뒤 모두에 위치할 수 있으며, 어느 위치에 있든 문장의 의미는 그대로 유지됩니다.
> 단, 시간 부사절이 주절 앞에 오는 경우 comma(,)를 반드시 부사절 끝에 붙여야 합니다.
>
> **When Mrs. Kim comes back**, I will tell her. = I will tell Mrs. Kim **when she comes back**.

2 시간 순서

아래 각 예문에서 어떤 일이 더 먼저 일어 났는지 알아봅시다.

● **When / After** I finish my project, I will take a holiday.

1. I finish the project.
2. I take a holiday.

● **Before** my friends come, I will clean my room.

1. I clean the room.
2. My friends come.

● **While** you are on vacation, I will take your messages.

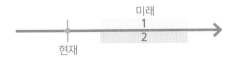

1. You are on vacation.
2. I take your messages.

Exercise

A **Underline the time clauses in the sentences. Then, write 1 if the underlined part happens first and write 2 if the underlined part happens second.**

> **Example** She will visit her friends in Florida <u>after she finishes her final paper.</u>
> 1

1. When she has an interview, she will do great.

2. He will come back to his office before his manager comes.

3. After she gets a job, she will save money.

4. I will help you when I have time next week.

5. Before the summer vacation starts, I will lose weight.

6. When I go to Australia, I will definitely go to Bondi beach.

7. I will finish my report before the boss yells at me.

8. He will take a bus after he gets off the subway.

B Fill in the blanks with the correct tense forms of the verbs given.

> **Example** They (make) __will make__ a Christmas tree before Christmas (come)
> __comes__ .

1. The salesperson (call) _____ you before she (get off) _____ from work.

2. When my friends (visit) _____ my hometown, I (show) _____ them around.

3. After Eunice(become) _____ a famous star, she (need) _____ a bodyguard.

4. While they (be) _____ in Beijing, they (visit) _____ the Great Wall.

5. When he (get) _____ the job, he (celebrate) _____ it with his family.

6. Before I (get) _____ married, I (travel) _____ around the world.

7. We (throw) _____ a surprise party when my dad (come) _____ home tonight.

8. Susan (go) _____ to bed right after she (finish) _____ her homework.

C Combine the two sentences into one using time clauses.

Example They are going to get married. Then they will move to New York.

➡ _They will move to New York after they get married_

1. I will come back at 12. Then I will talk to you.

   ➡ _____ after _____.

2. We will be in Hong Kong. We will enjoy the night view.

   ➡ While _____, _____.

3. He will look for a new job. Then he will quit his job

   ➡ Before _____, _____.

4. We will get there. We will stay in a youth hostel.

   ➡ _____ when _____.

5. You will be away. I will be busy with the term paper.

   ➡ While _____, _____.

6. I will warm up. Then I will go for a run.

   ➡ _____ before _____.

7. You will be back from the business trip. I will buy you dinner.

   ➡ When _____, _____.

Let's Speak!

14-3. mp3

Activity-1

A Listen to the conversations and check (√) if the following statements are true or false. 🎧

		True	False
1	• Erica will go to the hospital if she takes a day off.	☐	☐
	• Jason will have a party if he takes a day off.	☐	☐
2	• Hana will lead the team strictly if she becomes a manager.	☐	☐
	• Adam will be angry if his team members are late.	☐	☐
3	• Hailey will still love her boyfriend if her boyfriend cheats on her.	☐	☐
	• Sean will have a talk with the guy if his girlfriend cheats on him.	☐	☐

B With a partner, practice speaking by talking about what you will do in the following situations. Use future time clauses.

1. What will you do if you take a day off?

2. What will you do if you become a manager?

3. What will you do if you win a cash prize?

> **Example** **Q**: What will you do if you take a day off?
> **A**: If I take a day off, I will _____ go to my hometown _____.

Activity-2

A With a partner, practice speaking by playing the chain game. First, make a sentence starting with an *if clause*. Then, your partner must make a new sentence by using the main clause from your sentence to make an *if clause*. Take turns making sentences until one of you gives up.

> **Example**
> **A**: If I graduate from high school, _I will go to college_ .
> **B**: _If I go to college_ , I will study very hard.
> **A**: _If I study very hard_ , I will...

Activity-3

A With a partner, practice speaking by taking turns making sentences using the words given. Use future time clauses and make your own main clauses.

1. when / get home
2. before / get old
3. while / be on vacation
4. after / take a shower
5. before / go to work
6. if / win the lottery
7. after / get married
8. if / lose one's job
9. when / travel abroad
10. if / have no money at all

> **Example**   when / get home
> **A**: _I will cook dinner_ when I get home.
> **B**: _I will watch TV_ when I get home.

UNIT 15

Adjectives and Adverbs

형용사와 부사

PART 1   She is a smart cat.

Get Started

15-1. mp3

Read and listen to the dialogue.

Christine : Wow, that's a **beautiful** cat!

Kevin : That's Minky. She's a **Persian** cat.

Christine : Can I pick her up?

Kevin : Of course.

Christine : She is so **adorable**.

Kevin : Yes, she is. She is a **smart** cat too.

Focus

형용사 (Adjectives)

● 형용사는 사람 또는 사물의 성질, 상태, 수량 등을 부가 설명해주는 말로 명사를 수식하거나 보어의 역할을 합니다.

1 형용사의 역할

① 명사 수식

● 명사 앞: 명사 바로 앞에서 해당 명사에 부가적인 뜻을 더해줍니다.

There is a **cute** rabbit.

Look at the **tall, handsome** guy.   [형용사+명사]

She is wearing a **bright green** sweater.

● 명사 뒤: -thing 으로 끝나는 명사를 수식하는 경우 형용사는 이 명사 뒤에 위치합니다.

Did you hear anything **strange**?

I brought something **new** and **useful**.   [명사+형용사]

214 Unit 15 · Adjectives and Adverbs

② 보어 역할

● 형용사는 be 동사 뒤에 위치하여 주어를 설명하는 주격보어 역할을 하기도 합니다.

That rabbit is cute.

Kimchi is red and spicy.

[주어(명사)+be 동사+형용사]

2 형용사의 종류

① 기분 또는 상태를 나타내는 형용사

beautiful	happy	scary	delicious	ugly
intelligent	hard	clever	expensive	busy
handsome	kind	difficult	cute	lovely

② 크기, 모양, 색깔, 소재 등을 나타내는 형용사

size	age	shape	color
big	new	round	colorful
tall	old	flat	red
little	young	square	black
small		wide	white

Exercise

A **Underline the adjectives and circle the nouns that the adjectives modify in the sentences.**

Example   Do you know the tall man over there?

1. Your dress is very pretty and unique.

2. Peter is my old friend.

3. She has brown eyes.

4. Susan has long black hair.

5. I didn't find anything strange in the room.

6. There isn't anything exciting here.

7. I need something unusual for the party.

8. There are many fancy restaurants in this town.

9. Rick bought an expensive car and a huge house.

10. The sushi in the restaurant is very fresh, and the prices are reasonable.

B Put the adjectives given in the correct positions in the sentences. Add '*and*' where needed.

> **Example** There is a pen. (red)
>   ∧
>   red   nice and
>   ∨
>   Today's weather is warm. (nice)

1. She is wearing a dress. (long)

2. Professor Dickinson gave me a grade. (poor)

3. This cup is big. (round)

4. I love Mexican food. (spicy)

5. He has short hair. (blond)

6. All the people here are friendly. (clever)

C Fill in the blanks by putting the adjectives given in the correct order.

> **Example** (sunny / beautiful) ➡ The city has ___beautiful sunny___ weather.

1. (quiet / peaceful) ⇒ Sunday mornings are always _____ and
   _____.

2. (big / fancy) ⇒ We went to a _____ restaurant.

3. (brown / curly) ⇒ Eunice has _____ hair.

4. (little / cute) ⇒ Look at this _____ baby.

5. (gentle / Turkish) ⇒ I met a _____ man at the meeting.

6. (black / leather) ⇒ I bought a _____ jacket yesterday.

7. (sweet / cold) ⇒ I'd like to drink something _____ and
   _____.

8. (small / cozy) ⇒ I have a _____ house.

Get Started

15-2. mp3

Read and listen to the dialogue.

Helen : Thanks for inviting me to dinner, Chris.

Chris : You're welcome. By the way, you **look great** tonight.

Helen : You **look** quite **handsome**, too.

Chris : Thank you.

Helen : So, have you been to this buffet before?

Chris : No, it's my first time. People say the food here **tastes very good**.

Helen : Yeah, the food **smells delicious**.

Chris : Should we start at the salad bar?

Helen : That **sounds fantastic**.

Focus

▌ 지각동사(feel, look, sound, smell, taste)＋형용사

- 형용사는 지각동사 (Sense Verbs) 다음에도 위치할 수 있습니다.

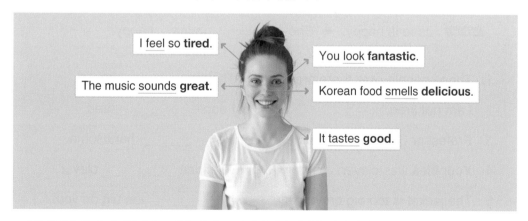

I feel so **tired**.

The music sounds **great**.

You look **fantastic**.

Korean food smells **delicious**.

It tastes **good**.

- 다음 문장을 통해 지각동사가 쓰였을 때와 be 동사가 사용되었을 때의 의미 차이를 비교해 보세요.

I **am** tired.	vs.	I **look** tired. ▎ I **feel** tired.
The music **is** great.	vs.	The music **sounds** great.
Korean food **is** delicious.	vs.	Korean food **looks** delicious. ▎ Korean food **smells** delicious. ▎ Korean food **tastes** delicious. ▎ Korean food **sounds** delicious.

Exercise

A Match the sentences with appropriate sense verb and adjectives.

	Sense Verbs	Adjectives

Example

My boss complimented me. I

1. I like your wedding dress. You

2. Have you tried Indian food? It

3. I like your idea. It

4. Are those roses? They

- look(s)
- sound(s)
- feel(s)
- taste(s)
- smell(s)

- delicious.
- fabulous.
- great.
- good.
- brilliant.

B Fill in the blanks with the correct forms of the sense verbs from the box.

look	sound	feel	taste	smell

Example Jane is happy. → She _looks_ / _sounds_ happy.

1. Those people over there are rich. → They _____ rich.

2. I am not tired. → I don't _____ tired.

3. Professor Geller is handsome. → He _____ handsome.

4. Your idea was clever. → The idea _____ clever.

5. The jacket is too big on you. → It _____ too big on you.

6. Columbian coffee is really good. → It _____/_____ really good.

7. Amy is shocked. → She _____ shocked.

8. Italian food is delicious. → Italian food _____/_____/
_____/_____ delicious.

Get Started 🎧

15-3. mp3

Read and listen to the dialogue.

Joseph: How was your weekend?

Andrea: It **was relaxing**. How was yours?

Joseph: It wasn't great.

Andrea: Why?

Joseph: I asked Amy out on Saturday, but she turned me down. So I **was depressed** for the whole weekend.

Andrea: Oh, I'm sorry to hear that.

Focus

▌분사 형용사 (Participial Adjectives)

● 분사 형용사는 현재 분사(-ing) 또는 과거 분사(-ed)가 문장에서 형용사처럼 사용되는 경우를 일컫습니다.

1 현재 분사 형용사: 동사원형+-ing

● 현재 분사 형용사는 사물을 묘사할 때 사용합니다.

Be Verb / Sense Verb + Present Participle	Present Participle + Noun
The movie was **boring**.	They watched a **boring** movie.
The question sounds **puzzling**.	He hated the **puzzling** question.

2 과거 분사 형용사: 동사원형+-ed

● 과거 분사 형용사는 사람이 어떤 사물에 대해 어떻게 느끼는지를 묘사할 때 사용됩니다.

Be Verb / Sense Verb + Past Participle	Past Participle + Noun
The children felt **bored**.	The **bored** children started screaming.
(because of the **boring** movie)	
He was so **puzzled**.	The **puzzled** man couldn't answer the question.
(because of the **puzzling** question)	

3 자주 사용하는 분사 형용사

Present Participial Adjectives		Past Participial Adjectives	
boring	pleasing	bored	pleased
confusing	relaxing	confused	relaxed
depressing	surprising	depressed	surprised
embarrassing	shocking	embarrassed	shocked
exciting	tiring	excited	tired
interesting	amazing	interested	amazed

Exercise

A Underline the participial adjectives in the sentences.

> **Example** I'm <u>tired</u> today.

1. The news was very surprising to me.

2. Jody was confused by the directions.

3. I felt depressed after I saw the movie.

4. Julian had a tiring weekend.

5. The soccer match was very exciting.

6. I had a relaxing weekend.

7. Did you hear the shocking news today?

8. Christine is an interesting person.

B Circle the correct answers.

Example They usually play ((exciting)/ excited) music.

1. The (shocking / shocked) news is on TV now.

2. Sorry for the (confusing / confused) information.

3. Everybody was happy with the (pleased / pleasing) news.

4. The (tired / tiring) people began to complain about the tour schedule.

5. The movie was so (touching / touched).

6. The show was very (surprising / surprised) to me.

7. Carrie is (interesting / interested) in science.

8. Mark and Pat felt so (boring / bored) at home.

C Complete the e-mail with the correct forms of the words given.

| send | To: | chris@hmail.com |

Dear Chris,

I have good news. Don't be (surprise) _____!!

I finally got a job at the *New York Times*!!
Isn't this (excite) _____? I'm so (please)
_____. You know, I was so (depress)
_____ when I didn't hear from any companies. I
went through so many (embarrass) _____ moments
in job interviews, and I was not sure about my future.

Anyway, I feel very (relax) _____ now. Chris, I want
to thank you for all your help.

Take care and see you soon.

Sincerely,

Jody

et Started 🎧

15-4. mp3

Read and listen to the instructions.

Plain Omelet Recipe

① Beat two eggs in a bowl **carefully**.

② Add salt and hot water to the bowl and stir **quickly**.

③ Heat the oil **slowly** in a pan.

④ Pour the mixture into the pan and let it cook **slowly**.

⑤ When it is cooked **well**, take it out of the pan.

⑥ Serve **immediately** while it is hot.

Focus

▌ 부사 (Adverbs)

- 부사는 동사, 형용사, 또는 다른 부사를 수식하는 역할을 하며, 다른 품사에 비해 문장에서 위치가 자유롭습니다.

She drives a car.

She drives a car **carefully**.
       ↑   Adverb

She **carefully** drives a car.
Adverb   ↑

⅂ 동사를 수식하는 부사

형용사+**-ly** 형태	slow → slowly	finally, suddenly, slowly, beautifully, carefully, quickly, badly, regularly, rapidly, loudly, immediately, wonderfully, correctly, quietly, softly
예외	happy → happily	lazily, luckily, easily, hastily, angrily
	late → late (형용사와 부사의 형태가 같은 경우)	fast, hard, early
	good → well	

2 형용사나 다른 부사를 수식하는 부사: very, really, extremely

● 이러한 부사들은 형용사나 다른 부사 앞에 위치하여 그 어휘를 수식합니다.

She is a **very** careful driver. | She drives **very** carefully.

형용사 수식　　　　　　　　　부사 수식

Exercise

A Underline the adverbs and circle the verbs that the adverbs modify in the sentences.

> **Example**　The man (walked) into the office quietly.

1. They always dress badly.

2. Tim happily waited for the concert.

3. I opened the door slowly.

4. John and Simon left early.

5. Jenny answered correctly.

6. The dog barked loudly when the man entered the house.

7. Linda and Henry angrily argued over the matter.

B Fill in the blanks with the adverbs of the words given.

> **Example**　She (quick) _quickly_ ran into the house.

1. He woke up (early) _____ this morning.

2. I opened the box (immediate) _____.

3. Cathy plays the guitar (excellent) _____.

4. Christina looked back (angry) _____.

5. Steven drives (fast) _____.

6. Dan goes to the gym (regular) _____.

7. The children behave (bad) _____.

8. We decorated the Christmas tree (beautiful) _____.

C Rewrite the sentences by using appropriate adverbs from the box.

Example   He played the guitar. ➡ He played the guitar excellently.

skillfully	unfortunately	honestly	well
very	strongly	quickly	beautifully

1. Emily swims. ➡ _____

2. I learn things. ➡ _____

3. The wind blows. ➡ _____

4. It began to rain. ➡ _____

5. It was hot yesterday. ➡ _____

6. Gary speaks English. ➡ _____

7. She danced at the contest. ➡ _____

8. James answered my questions. ➡ _____

D Read the sentences and fill in the blanks with the correct adjectives.

Example   She drives carefully. ➡ She is a   careful   driver.

1. Mark runs fast.
    ➡ Mark is a _____ runner.

2. Jon acts badly in the movie.
    ➡ Jon is a _____ actor.

3. My father cooks very well.
    ➡ My father is a _____ cook.

4. Ella dances gracefully.
    ➡ Ella is a _____ dancer.

5. Susie works hard.
    ➡ Susie is a _____ worker.

E **Read the sentences and fill in the blanks with the correct adverbs.**

Example Abby is a wonderful singer. ➡ Abby sings _wonderfully_ .

1. Ron is a heavy smoker.
   ➡ Ron smokes _____ .

2. Ken is a lazy worker.
   ➡ Ken works _____ .

3. Kelly is a quiet talker.
   ➡ Kelly talks _____ .

4. Dave is an excellent soccer player.
   ➡ Dave plays soccer _____ .

5. Greg and Susan are fluent French speakers.
   ➡ Greg and Susan speak French _____ .

PART 5 — She checks her e-mail every morning.

Get Started 🎧

15-5. mp3

Read and listen to the passage.

Julia's Routine

Julia **usually** gets up at 6:00 am. She **always** takes a shower in the morning and she **rarely** has breakfast. She **always** takes the subway to work. She **sometimes** reads a book on the subway.

She checks her e-mails **every morning**. She works out **twice a week**, and she goes hiking **once a month**. She goes to church **every Sunday**.

Focus

▌ 빈도 부사 (Frequency Adverbs)

- 행동이나 사건의 빈도 또는 횟수를 나타내는 부사를 말합니다.

never	rarely	sometimes	often	usually	always

0% ⟵——————————————————————————⟶ 100%

- 빈도 부사의 위치

일반 동사 앞				Be 동사, 조동사 뒤		
He	never rarely sometimes often usually always	gets up	early.	He	is will	never rarely sometimes often usually always	busy. be busy.

0% ⟶ 100%

▌ 빈도를 나타내는 표현 (Frequency Expressions)

- 행동이나 사건의 빈도 또는 횟수를 나타내는 표현을 말합니다.

every morning	every night	every day	once a week
twice a week	three times a year	every Sunday	on Mondays

● 빈도를 나타내는 표현의 위치: 주로 문장 끝에 위치하며, 때에 따라 문장 시작 부분에 위치하기도 합니다.

	every morning.	
He goes jogging	every night.	Every morning, he goes jogging.
	once a week.	
	twice a month.	

Exercise

A Rewrite the sentences by putting the words given in the correct positions.

> **Example** I clean my room on the weekend. (usually)
>
> ➡ I ___usually___ clean my room on the weekend.

1. I visit my grandmother. (often)

   ➡ _____

2. They get to work on time. (always)

   ➡ _____

3. He is serious. (never)

   ➡ _____

4. He makes a mistake. (rarely)

   ➡ _____

5. I read books before going to bed. (sometimes)

   ➡ _____

6. I am at the office in the morning. (usually)

   ➡ _____

7. We eat food late at night. (sometimes)

   ➡ _____

8. John says bad things about other people. (never)

   ➡ _____

B Look at the calendar and complete the sentences with the correct frequency expressions from the box.

Chris's Habits

Sun	Mon	Tue	Wed	Thu	Fri	Sat
1 👟	2	3 👟	4	5 👟	6 🍽	7 🧺
8 👕	9 👟	10	11 👟	12	13 🍽👟	14 🧺
15 👟	16 👟	17	18 👕	19 👟	20 🍽	21 🧺
22 👟	23	24 😎	25 👟	26 👟	27 🍽	28 🧺

once a month	twice a month	three times a month
three times a week	every Saturday	every Friday
every Wednesday		

 = go for a walk   = eat out   = take a day off

 = go shopping for clothes   = do the laundry

1. Chris goes for a walk _____.

2. Chris does the laundry _____.

3. Chris eats out _____.

4. Chris takes a day off _____.

5. Chris goes shopping for clothes _____.

C Rewrite the sentences by using the frequency adverbs and the frequency expressions given.

> Example I go to the movies. (every Friday)

> ➡   _I go to the movies every Friday._

1. I brush my teeth. (every night)

   ➡ _____

2. I do the laundry. (once a week)

   ➡ _____

3. I take a walk in the park with my sister. (often, in the morning)

   ➡ _____

4. I go to a bar. (usually, at night)

   ➡ _____

5. Mary works. (never, on the weekend)

   ➡ _____

6. Jake checks his e-mails. (always, before midnight)

   ➡ _____

7. My family gets together. (usually, twice a year)

   ➡ _____

8. I go to the library with my friend. (sometimes, on Sunday)

   ➡ _____

Let's Speak!

Activity-1

A Listen to the three descriptions of each picture and choose the one description that does not match each picture. 🎧

1.   □a □b □c

2.   □a □b □c

3.   □a □b □c

4.   □a □b □c

Activity-2

B With a partner, practice speaking by taking turns describing the following items to each other. If your partner guesses wrong, give more descriptions until he/she gets it right. Use the words from the box to describe the items.

dining table	laptop	pencil	ring
smart phone	coffee bean	cheese	lemon

Example
A : It is oval and brown.
B : Is it a dining table?
A : No, it isn't. It is small and smells nice.
B : Is it a coffee bean?
A : That's right.

Activity-3

A Listen to the short conversations and put the numbers of the conversations in the correct pictures.

A.

B.

C.

D.

Activity-4

A With a partner, practice speaking by describing one of your family members to each other. Use the words from the boxes and/or your own words.

Adjectives	Verbs	Adverbs
pretty, handsome, cute, ugly, intelligent, kind, lovely, slim, chubby, tall, long, wavy, curly, …	dance, swim, run, sing, cook, talk, learn, speak, study, …	beautifully, loudly, wonderfully, well, fast, hard, quickly, …

Example My younger sister is 20 years old. Her name is Lena. She is **very pretty** and has **long curly** hair. She dances **wonderfully**, and she cooks **well**…

Activity - 5

A With a partner, practice speaking by taking turns asking and answering how often you do the following things. Use frequency adverbs and complete sentences to answer the questions.

> **Example** **A**: How often do you use the Internet?
> **B**: I use the Internet every day.

1. use the Internet

2. read the news online

3. write e-mails

4. use Internet banking

5. play online games

6. chat online

7. buy clothes online

8. listen to music online

9. buy books online

UNIT 16
Comparatives and Superlatives
비교급과 최상급

PART 1 Your bag is bigger than mine.

Get Started

16-1. mp3

Read and listen to the dialogue.

Sarah： Good morning, Jessica.

Jessica： Hi, Sarah. Is that a new bag?

Sarah： Yes, it is. I just got it yesterday.

Jessica： It looks similar to mine.

Sarah： But your bag is **bigger than** mine.

Jessica： Yeah, but mine looks **less expensive than** yours.

Sarah： That's only because your bag is **older than** mine.

Jessica： Yeah, I should get a new bag soon.

Focus

▌비교급 (Comparatives)

- 비교급에는 크게 형용사의 비교급과 부사의 비교급이 있으며, 이는 두 가지 사물 또는 두 사람을 서로 비교할 때 사용됩니다.

1 형용사의 비교급

① 형태: 형용사+-er, more+형용사(더 ~한) / less+형용사(덜 ~한)

Rules	Examples	
1음절 형용사+-er	tall → taller	old → older
1음절 [단모음+자음] 순서로 끝난 형용사: 마지막 자음 반복+-er	big → bigger	hot → hotter
2음절 이상의 형용사: 형용사 앞에 more / less	difficult → **more** difficult expensive → **less** expensive	
2음절이라도 [자음+y]로 끝난 형용사: y → i+-er	pretty → prettier	friendly → friendlier
불규칙 변화	good → **better** little → **less**	bad → **worse** many, much → **more**

② 문장 구조: A+be 동사+형용사의 비교급+than+B [A가 B 보다 더/덜 ~하다]

Tom is taller than Jason.

Ron is older than Katie.

That classroom is bigger than this classroom.

Inside is hotter than outside.

I think roses are prettier than Tulips.

Anna is friendlier than Cathy.

Math is more difficult than languages.

That wallet is less expensive than this wallet.

Megan's painting is better than yours.

Peter's report is worse than Tyler's.

2 부사의 비교급

① 형태: 부사+-er, more+부사(더 ~하게)/less+부사(덜 ~하게)

Rules	Examples	
-ly로 끝나는 부사: 부사 앞에 more / less	quickly → more quickly frequently → less frequently 예외 early → earlier	
-ly로 끝나지 않는 부사: 부사 뒤에 -er	fast → faster	hard → harder
불규칙 변화	well → better little → less	badly → worse much → more

② 문장구조: A+일반동사+부사의 비교급+than+B [A가 B 보다 더/덜 ~하다]

She finishes her work more quickly than I (do).

He drives more carefully than his brother.

She always arrives earlier than her manager.

Eric runs faster than Ron.

Susan works harder than Fiona.

He always arrives later than his manager.

Megan dances better than you.

Peter sings worse than Tyler.

Exercise

Ⓐ Write the correct comparative forms of the adjectives/adverbs.

Example thick _thicker_

1. soft	_____	2. smart	_____	3. heavy	_____
4. dirty	_____	5. small	_____	6. delicious	_____
7. bright	_____	8. ugly	_____	9. handsome	_____
10. new	_____	11. slowly	_____	12. late	_____
13. easily	_____	14. early	_____	15. well	_____
16. fast	_____	17. badly	_____	18. little	_____
19. interesting	_____	20. fluently	_____	21. hard	_____
22. many	_____	23. quickly	_____		

Ⓑ Look at the pictures and complete the sentences by using the correct comparative forms of the given adjectives/adverbs.

1.

Example

delicious

Q: The ice cream is _more delicious_ _than_ the bread.

J'aime bien le cinema!

Uh...

fluently

Helen speaks French _____ _____ John.

2.

fast

The rabbit runs _____ _____ the turtle.

3.

good

Today, I feel _____ _____ yesterday.

4.

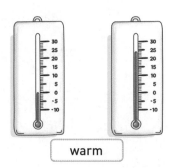

warm

Florida is _____ Chicago.

5.

badly

Peter did _____ Robert on the math test.

6.

expensive

The black car is _____ _____ the white car.

7.

carefully

Claire listens to the lecture _____ _____ Andy.

C Write sentences about Mark and Don using the comparative forms of the words given.

Mark says...	Don says...
I am 180cm tall. I have short curly hair. I weigh 68kg. I am 25 years old.	I am 175cm tall. I have long straight hair. I weigh 80kg. I am 35 years old.

1. Mark is _____. (tall)

2. Mark's hair is _____. (short)

3. Don is _____. (heavy)

4. Don is _____. (old)

He is the strongest person in the class.

Get Started

16-2. mp3

Read and listen to the dialogue.

Holly : Did you hear about the fight?

Tim : No, what fight?

Holly : Brian had a fight with Chris, and Chris got a black eye.

Tim : I can't believe it. Brian is **the weakest person** in the class.

Holly : Right. How did he beat Chris? He **is the strongest person** in the class.

Tim : I know. It's **the most shocking** news ever.

Focus

▌최상급 (Superlatives)

● 비교급과 마찬가지로 최상급에는 형용사의 최상급과 부사의 최상급이 있으며, 이는 셋 또는 그 이상의 사물 또는 사람 가운데 어떤 하나가 도드라지는 점을 나타낼 때 사용됩니다.

1 형용사의 최상급

① 형태: 형용사+-est, most+형용사(가장 ~한) / least+형용사(가장 덜 ~한)

Rules	Examples
1음절 형용사+-est -e로 끝나는 형용사+-st	young → young**est** tall → tall**est** large → large**st**
1음절 [단모음+자음]으로 끝나는 형용사: 마지막 자음 반복+-est	big → big**gest** hot → hot**test**
2음절 이상 형용사: 형용사 앞에 most / least	difficult → **most** difficult interesting → **least** interesting
2음절이라도 [자음+y]로 끝나는 형용사: y → i+-est	pretty → prett**iest** friendly → friendl**iest**
불규칙 변화	good → **best** bad → **worst** little → **least** many, much → **most**

② 문장 구조: A+be 동사+the+형용사의 최상급 [A가 가장 ~하다]

David is the youngest in my family.

Susie is the tallest in my class.

Tokyo is the largest city in Japan.

That was the biggest mistake of my life.

August is the hottest month of the year.

Joy is the prettiest student in my class.

Anna is the friendliest among all my friends.

I think physics is the most difficult subject.

I think *Moby Dick* is the least interesting novel on the list.

Megan is the best dancer in the world.

Peter's report is the worst in our department.

2 부사의 최상급

① 형태: 부사+-est, most+부사(가장 ~하게)/least+부사(가장 덜 ~하게)

Rules	Examples	
-ly로 끝나지 않는 부사+-est	hard → hard**est**	late → lat**est**
-ly로 끝나는 부사: 부사 앞에 most/least	carefully → **most** carefully frequently → **least** frequently 예외 early → earli**est**	
불규칙 변화	well → best little → least	badly → worst much → most

② 문장구조: A+일반동사+the+부사의 최상급 [A가 가장 ~하게 …하다]

Brandon worked the hardest in class.

The plane to Chicago leaves the earliest of the three planes.

My younger brother drives the most carefully among us.

Megan dances the best in the world.

Peter sings the worst in our department.

Exercise

A Write the correct superlative forms of the adjectives / adverbs.

> **Example** fast _____fastest_____

1. hard _____
2. early _____
3. young _____
4. expensive _____
5. happy _____
6. rich _____
7. happily _____
8. handsome _____
9. useful _____
10. friendly _____
11. hot _____
12. loud _____
13. lazy _____
14. interesting _____
15. slowly _____
16. big _____
17. dangerous _____
18. shiny _____
19. fluently _____
20. good _____
21. badly _____
22. much _____
23. little _____

B Fill in the blanks with the correct superlative forms of the words given.

> Example   That was (- delicious) _the least delicious_ chicken.

1. The Nile is (+long) _____ river in the world.

2. Yesterday was (+bad) _____ day of my life.

3. My younger sister drives (- carefully) _____ in my family.

4. She sings (+well) _____ in the church choir.

5. Andy did things (+slowly) _____ in the department.

6. Gary works (+hard) _____ among his team.

7. It's (+expensive) _____ hotel in Seoul.

8. Japanese is (+easy) _____ foreign language for Koreans.

9. Today's meeting was (+boring) _____ meeting so far this week.

10. This novel was (- interesting) _____ book among the three novels.

C Make sentences using the superlative form of the words given.

Example be / fluent / English / speaker

→ Tracy   is the most fluent English speaker.

1. be / delightful / person

   → Alex _____

2. be / lazy / worker

   → Edgar _____

3. be / funny / friend

   → Anna _____

4. speak / loud

   → Nicole _____

5. work / hard

   → Megan _____

6. be / careful / driver

   → Rachel _____

7. spend / much / money

   → Peter _____

8. play / the piano / well

   → Joseph _____

Let's Speak!

Activity - 1

A Listen to the recordings and write the correct answers in the blanks. Then, with a partner, practice speaking by asking and answering the questions. Make sure to use comparative sentences to answer the questions. 🎧

1
(1) Who is older, Ryan or Derrick? _____
(2) Who plays sports better, Ryan or Derrick? _____
(3) Who is more boring, Ryan or Derrick? _____

2
(1) Who is younger, John or Chris? _____
(2) Who weighs more, John or Chris? _____
(3) Who is more outgoing, John or Chris? _____
(4) Who studies harder, John or Chris? _____

3
(1) Who is older? Linda or David? _____
(2) Who works faster, Linda or David? _____
(3) Who gets to work earlier, Linda or David? _____
(4) Who argues more with Chris, Linda or David? _____

Example **A :** Who is older, Ryan or Derrick?
B : _____ is older than _____ .

Activity-2

(A) The following describes some characteristics of men and women. Write comparative sentences using the information given and check (✓) whether or not you agree with the statements. Then, ask your partner questions about the statements and check your partner's answers.

Men	Women
• realistic	• idealistic
• good at science / math	• good at languages
• get stressed out often	• get depressed often
• do not listen carefully	• listen carefully
• do not ask for help easily	• ask for help easily

	You		Your Partner	
	Agree	Disagree	Agree	Disagree
1. Men are more realistic than women.	☐	☐	☐	☐
2.	☐	☐	☐	☐
3.	☐	☐	☐	☐
4.	☐	☐	☐	☐
5.	☐	☐	☐	☐
6.	☐	☐	☐	☐
7.	☐	☐	☐	☐
8.	☐	☐	☐	☐
9.	☐	☐	☐	☐
10.	☐	☐	☐	☐

Example **A:** Do you think men are more realistic than women?
B: Yes, I think so. / No. I think women are more realistic than men.

Activity - 3

A With a partner, practice speaking by asking and answering questions using superlatives and the words given. Use the words from the box to answer some of the questions.

- what / tall / building / world
- what / long / river / world
- what / big / city / world
- what / high / mountain / world
- what / beautiful / place to visit / world
- who / famous / actor / Hollywood
- who / good / singer / your country
- who / important / person / your country's history
- who / successful / person / around you
- who / popular / student / class
- when / good / time / of year

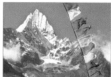

> **Example** **A** : What is the tallest building in the world?
> **B** : I think the Burj Khalifa is the tallest building in the world.

| The Nile River | Mount Everest | Christmas | Burj Khalifa | Beijing |

UNIT 17
Infinitives and Gerunds
부정사와 동명사

PART 1 I'd like to get a new shirt.

Get Started

Read and listen to the dialogue.

David : I'm going to go to the mall **to get a new shirt**.

Carrie : What do you need a new shirt for?

David : I have a blind date, so I'**d like to look** neat and stylish.

Carrie : Do you **want me to go** shopping with you?

David : That would be great. **It's not easy to shop** for clothes alone.

Carrie : I have a good feeling about your blind date.

David : Thanks. I **hope to meet** the right girl for me this time.

Focus

▌To 부정사(To-infinitive): to+동사원형

- To 부정사는 [to+동사원형]의 형태로 문장에서 명사 또는 부사와 같은 역할을 합니다. 이를 각각 to 부정사의 명사적 용법, 부사적 용법이라고 부르는데, 아래에서 예문을 통해 그 역할을 자세히 살펴봅시다.

1 To 부정사의 명사적 용법

- To 부정사가 명사적 용법으로 쓰일 때는 명사처럼 문장에서 주어, 보어 또는 목적어 자리에 와서 명사의 역할을 대신합니다.

① 동사의 목적어와 보어 역할

	would like, want, agree, hope, learn, need, decide, plan, like + to 부정사 목적어
동사+ to 부정사	He likes **to play** basketball. 그는 농구하는 것을 좋아한다. 　　　　목적어 역할
	She decided not **to take** a bus. 그녀는 버스를 타지 않기로 결심했다. 　　　　　　목적어 역할

동사+목적어+ to 부정사	**want, ask, tell, would like, expect, order,** **invite, encourage, allow, enable, warn, teach** ＋ 목적어 ＋ **to** 부정사 목적격 보어
	The manager wants me **to finish** the report today. <u>목적격 보어 역할</u> 매니저는 내가 오늘까지 보고서를 마무리하기를 원한다. I told her not **to stay** up late. <u>목적격 보어 역할</u> 나는 그녀에게 늦게까지 깨어있지 말라고 했다.

② 문장의 주어 역할

● To 부정사가 문장에서 주어의 역할을 할 경우, 보통 to 부정사를 대신하여 it이 문장의 제일 앞 주어의 자리에 위치하고 to 부정사는 문장의 뒤쪽에 위치하게 됩니다.

It is＋보어＋ to 부정사	**It is** hard **to make** a good friend. 좋은 친구를 사귀는 것은 어렵다. <u>주어 역할</u> **It is** fun **to watch** cartoons. 만화를 보는 것은 즐겁다. <u>주어 역할</u>

2 To 부정사의 부사적 용법

● To 부정사는 문장 내에서 부사의 역할을 하여 동사나 문장 전체에 목적(~하기 위해)이나 이유(~하게 되어)의 뜻을 덧붙여 줍니다.

목적	She runs 5 km a day **to lose** weight. 그녀는 살을 빼기 위하여 매일 5km를 달린다. = Why does she run 5 km a day? - To lose weight He went to the store **to buy** a toothbrush. 그는 칫솔을 사기 위해 가게에 갔다. = Why did he go to the store? - To buy a toothbrush
이유	I am sorry **to hear** about the sad news. 슬픈 소식을 듣게 되어 유감이야. = Why are you sorry? - Because I heard about the sad news He was happy **to hear** from Amy. Amy로부터 소식을 듣게 되어 그는 기뻤다. = Why was he happy? - Because he heard from Amy

Exercise

A Fill in the blanks with the to-infinitive forms of the verbs from the box.

| think | learn | exercise | visit | play | study | write |

Example I like __to exercise__ at the gym after work.

1. Some kids learn _____ the alphabet before entering school.

2. It is difficult _____ other languages.

3. I want _____ in English when I talk to foreigners.

4. When I'm in Venice, I'd like you _____ me.

5. My sister failed the test. I told her _____ harder next time.

6. Are you going to play basketball? I want _____ as well.

B Fill in the blanks with the to-infinitive forms of the verbs given. Write the objects of the main verbs where needed.

Example My boss asked (copy) __me to copy__ this document for her.

1. I plan (buy) _____ a new car next year.

2. Do you expect (see) _____ the president today?

3. We all hope (work) _____ with you again someday.

4. I'm so tired. I just want (go to bed) _____ early today.

5. She decided (lose) _____ weight.

6. He invited (have) _____ dinner with him tonight.

7. She told (be) _____ quiet during the meeting.

8. I would like (make) _____ a brief comment on this matter.

C Correct the errors in the sentences.

> Example I like her to play the piano.

1. He agreed stay late.

2. He told to answer the phone.

3. I hope see you soon.

4. I invited to come over to my house this weekend.

5. It is hard to telling the truth.

6. It is always good to saw you.

7. It is always exciting throw a party.

D Fill in the blanks with the correct forms of the verbs from the box.

| be sad / hear | be afraid / drive | be happy / see | be excited / go |
| study / pass | go / buy | get up / go | |

> Example We ___were excited to go___ to the amusement park yesterday.

1. I _____ the car after the accident.

2. I _____ the news about your grandmother.

3. I _____ all my friends at the party last week.

4. She always _____ early _____ to the gym.

5. Everybody _____ very hard _____ the exam.

6. Yesterday, he _____ to the supermarket _____ some milk.

I enjoyed swimming at the beach.

Get Started

17-2. mp3

Read and listen to the dialogue.

Gary: How was your weekend at the beach?

Cindy: It was really nice. I **enjoyed sunbathing and swimming.** How was yours?

Gary: Mine was horrible. I wanted to finish my paper before Monday, but my computer broke down.

Cindy: Why didn't you call David? He's **good at fixing** computers.

Gary: I did. I **kept calling,** but he didn't answer the phone. So I **stopped calling him.** Maybe he was away for the weekend.

Cindy: Oh, I see.

Focus

▌동명사 (Gerund)

● 동명사는 [동사원형+-ing]의 형태로 앞서 살펴본 to 부정사의 명사적 용법과 마찬가지로 문장에서 명사의 역할을 합니다.

1 동사의 목적어 역할

● To 부정사가 명사적 용법으로 쓰일 때는 명사처럼 문장에서 주어, 보어 또는 목적어 자리에 와서 명사의 역할을 대신합니다.

① 동사의 목적어 역할

동명사를 목적어로 취하는 동사	**enjoy, stop, finish, keep, mind, quit + 동명사 목적어**
	I enjoy **working** here. He didn't finish **writing** the essay.
to 부정사 / 동명사 둘 다 목적어로 취하는 동사	**like, love, prefer, start, begin, hate + 동명사 / to 부정사 목적어**
	I like **playing** basketball. I like **to play** basketball. She began **singing** in the church choir. She began **to sing** in the church choir.

2 전치사의 목적어 역할

[전치사+동명사]구	be good at -ing	I am good at **dancing**.
	be for -ing	This tool is for **cutting** trees.
	be interested in -ing	He is interested in **making** robots.
	talk about -ing	She is talking about **learning** English.
	be looking forward to -ing	I am looking forward to **seeing** you soon.
	think of -ing	They are thinking of **visiting** Tokyo.

Exercise

A Fill in the blanks with the gerund and/or the to-infinitive forms of the verbs given.

> **Example** He didn't enjoy (ski) ___skiing___ during weekends.

1. I quit (smoke) _____ for sure.

2. She likes (jog) _____ in the morning.

3. People started (spend) _____ more time outdoors these days.

4. Students need (review) _____ Chapters 6 to 12.

5. I enjoy (share) _____ food with somebody.

6. We began (talk) _____ about the problem.

7. My cousins kept (ask) _____ me questions.

8. Would you mind (open) _____ the window? It's hot in here.

B Circle the correct answers.

> Example   I don't want (to sleep / sleeping) tonight.

1. The professor kept (to talk / talking) until the end of class.

2. She learned (to play / playing) tennis.

3. He finally decided (to quit / quitting) his job.

4. Do you mind (to close / closing) the door?

5. We plan (to hold / holding) a surprise party for Jane.

6. They all finished (to write / writing) the reports before noon.

7. We enjoy (to watch / watching) horror movies at midnight.

8. I expected him (to give / giving) me a ride, but he didn't.

C Fill in the blanks with the correct forms of the verbs from the box.

search	bake	hear	take	go	sing	have

> Example   The choir was really good at ___singing___.

1. She is interested in _____ cakes.

2. They were talking about _____ skiing.

3. He thought of _____ Mexican food for dinner.

4. Jason is good at _____ photos.

5. The Internet is for _____ for information.

6. I'm looking forward to _____ from you soon.

Get Started 🎧

17-3 mp3

Read and listen to the dialogue.

Tom： Do you want a cigarette?

David： No, thanks. I quit smoking.

Tom： Wow, what **made you stop**?

David： My girlfriend **made me quit smoking**.

Tom： Really? My mother **had me stop smoking** once, but I couldn't quit for good.

David： You should **let her wish come true**. It's not that hard.

Focus

▌사역동사 (Causative Verbs): make, have, get, let

● make, have, get은 '~하게 만들다, 시키다'라는 뜻으로 쓰이며, let은 '~하는 것을 허락하다'라는 의미로 사용됩니다. 사역동사 make, have, let 다음에 오는 동사의 형태는 동사원형이며, get 다음에는 to 부정사가 옵니다. 다음에서 각 사역동사의 용법을 자세히 알아봅시다.

1 Make, have, get: ~로 하여금 …하게 만들다, 시키다

make＋object(사람)＋동사원형	She **made** me **sing** in front of many people. 그녀는 나로 하여금 많은 사람들 앞에서 노래를 부르게 하였다. My boss always **makes** me **make** coffee for him. 내 보스는 항상 나로 하여금 자기 커피를 타게 시킨다.
have＋object(사람)＋동사원형	I **had** the technician **check** my computer this morning. 나는 오늘 아침에 기술자가 내 컴퓨터를 점검하게 하였다. I **had** my younger brother **bring** me an umbrella. 나는 내 남동생에게 나한테 우산을 가져오라고 시켰다.
get＋object(사람)＋**to** 부정사	Jason **gets** his children **to read** many books. Jason은 그의 아이들이 책을 많이 읽게끔 한다. I **got** my roommate **to cook** dinner yesterday. 나는 어제 내 룸메이트가 저녁 식사를 요리하게 했다.

2 Let: ~가 …하는 것을 허락하다

let + object(사람) **+ 동사원형**	The police officer **let** me **go**. 그 경찰관은 내가 가는 것을 허락했다.
	My parents won't **let** me **sleep** over at my friend's house.
	우리 부모님은 내가 친구 집에서 자고 오는 것을 허락하지 않을 것이다.

> let이 긍정 평서문에서 사용될 때는, 다른 사역동사와는 달리 시제나 주어에 따라 형태가 변하지 않습니다.
>
> The police officer <u>letted</u> me go yesterday. (x)
> The police officer <u>lets</u> me go. (x)

Exercise

(A) Use the words and the causative verbs given to make sentences. Make sure to put the causative verbs in the correct positions.

> **Example** The teacher / me / read the passage aloud (make)
>
> → <u>The teacher made me read the passage aloud.</u>

1. My boss / me / go home early / yesterday (let)

   → _____

2. I / sometimes / my younger sister / get milk / on the way home (have)

   → _____

3. Ken / always / Cindy / set the alarm clock for 6 am (get)

   → _____

4. He / the waiter / bring / him / a glass of water / an hour ago (have)

   → _____

5. Professor Hanson / us / hand in / the final essay / next week (let)

   → _____

6. Mr. Carrey / his assistant / finish / the report / this morning (get)

   → _____

7. The security guard / didn't / us / enter / the building / before 9:30 am (let)

   → _____

8. My boyfriend / always / me / go home / early (make)

   → _____

B Correct the errors in the sentences.

Example   He let me ~~to~~ borrow his laptop during the class.

1. Eric got Mindy plan a ski trip this time.

2. The boss made us preparing for the tomorrow's seminar.

3. My physics teacher letted us take a break for a moment.

4. My housemate always makes me cooking dinner.

5. Yesterday, I had my assistant made a delivery for me.

6. My mother doesn't let me to open up the presents before Christmas.

7. The parents had their children to only eat homemade food.

8. I got the housekeeper clean up the room.

Let's Speak!

Activity-1

A With a partner, practice speaking by asking and answering questions using the words given.

| plan / go shopping for clothes | hope / go out for dinner | need / study hard for the final exams | like / go to pop concerts |

Example
A : What does she plan to do?
B : She plans to go shopping for clothes.

B With a partner, practice speaking by asking and answering questions using the words given.

| ask / give her a hand | tell / call him back | want / water the plants in the yard | expect / go to a movie with them |

Example
A : What did she ask you to do?
B : She asked me to give her a hand.

Activity-2

A Match the activities with the correct reasons. Then, with a partner, practice speaking by asking and answering questions using the information.

Activities	Reasons
Sally is running.	talk about his paper
Peter studies very hard.	take a Chinese course every morning
Alex went to see his professor.	get to the class on time
Vivian gets up early.	get some fresh air
Chelsea went outside.	pass the final test

Example

A : Why is Sally running?

B : She is running to get to the class on time.

Activity-3

(A) Complete the following questions using the to-infinitive/gerund forms of the verbs given.

Questions

1. Do you like (study) alone?
2. Would you like (ride) a motorcycle?
3. Do you enjoy (watch) horror movies?
4. Do you want (make) more money?
5. Did you start (work) early today?
6. Do you hope (live) in another country?
7. Do you enjoy (exercise) every day?
8. Did you learn (drive)?
9. Are you good at (cook)?
10. Are you interested in (study) foreign languages?

(B) Check (✓) your answers to the questions in A. Then, ask your partner these questions and check your partner's answers.

Questions	1	2	3	4	5	6	7	8	9	10
You	Yes ☐ No ☐	Yes ☐ No ☐	Yes ☐ No ☐	Yes ☐ No ☐	Yes ☐ No ☐	Yes ☐ No ☐	Yes ☐ No ☐	Yes ☐ No ☐	Yes ☐ No ☐	Yes ☐ No ☐
Your Partner	Yes ☐ No ☐	Yes ☐ No ☐	Yes ☐ No ☐	Yes ☐ No ☐	Yes ☐ No ☐	Yes ☐ No ☐	Yes ☐ No ☐	Yes ☐ No ☐	Yes ☐ No ☐	Yes ☐ No ☐

(C) Compare your answers with your partner's and talk about what you two have in common.

> **Example** I like to study alone, and my partner likes studying alone, too.

Activity-4

(A) Listen to the conversations and check (✓) the statements that are true. 🎧

1
Julie had Tim make 30 copies. ☐

Julie didn't let Tim type the document first. ☐

2
The professor made students hand in their reports by this month. ☐

The professor let students hand in their reports by next month. ☐

3
Ms. Kelly let Ron take a week off next month. ☐

Ms. Kelly didn't let Ron take a week off next month. ☐

4
Mom got Tom to go shopping for groceries. ☐

Mom got Tom to make the shopping list. ☐

UNIT 18

Present Perfect Tense

현재완료 시제

PART 1 Have you ever been to Disneyland?

Get Started 🎧

18-1. mp3

Read and listen to the dialogue.

Stranger: Excuse me. Could you help me? I want to buy a train ticket from this machine.

Youngmi: Of course. Press this button and… There you go.

Stranger: Thank you very much. By the way, you speak English very well. **Have you lived** in any English speaking country before?

Youngmi: **Yes, I've lived** in the U.S. before.

Stranger: Oh, I see. **Have you ever been** to Disneyland in the U.S.?

Youngmi: **No, I haven't.**

Focus

▌현재완료 시제 (Present Perfect Tense)

- 현재완료 시제는 과거의 경험을 나타내거나, 어떤 행동이 과거의 어떤 시점에서 시작되어 현재까지도 계속되고 있음을 나타낼 때 사용됩니다.
- 현재완료 시제에서 동사는 [have/has+동사의 과거분사형(Past Participle)]인 현재완료의 형태로 사용됩니다.

1. 동사의 과거분사형 (Past Participle)

① 규칙 동사(Regular Verbs)의 과거분사형: 과거형(past)과 동일한 형태로 동사의 원형에 -d/-ed를 붙인 형태
finished, stopped, visited, opened, played, lived

② 불규칙 동사(Irregular Verbs)의 과거분사형: 과거형(past)이 따로 존재하는 것처럼 과거분사형(past participle)도 별도로 존재

Base Verb	Past	Past Participle	Base Verb	Past	Past Participle
am / is / are	was / were	been	know	knew	known
do / does	did	done	make	made	made
begin	began	begun	meet	met	met
buy	bought	bought	read	read	read
come	came	come	ride	rode	ridden
draw	drew	drawn	run	ran	run
drink	drank	drunk	say	said	said
drive	drove	driven	see	saw	seen
eat	ate	eaten	sing	sang	sung
find	found	found	speak	spoke	spoken
fly	flew	flown	spend	spent	spent
forget	forgot	forgotten	take	took	taken
get	got	got	tell	told	told
give	gave	given	think	thought	thought
go	went	gone	write	wrote	written
have	had	had	win	won	won

2 현재완료 시제의 경험적 용법

- 과거의 어떤 시점으로부터 현재까지 경험한 적이 있는 사실을 나타낼 때 쓰이며, 흔히 before, often, never, once, twice 등의 표현과 함께 사용됩니다.

I **have traveled** around many countries before.
나는 예전에 많은 나라를 여행한 적이 있다.

Past — Now

① 긍정문 / 부정문(Affirmative / Negative Statements)

Subject	have / has	(not / never)	Past Participle	
I / You / They / We	have	(never / not)	driven	a Ferrari before.
He / She / It	has	(never / not)	tried	any Indian food before.

② Yes / No 의문문(Yes / No Questions and Short Answers)

- 주어와 과거분사형 사이에 ever를 넣어 경험(~한 적이 있나요?)의 의미를 나타낼 수 있습니다.

have / has	subject	ever	Past Participle	
Have	I / you / they / we	ever	lived	in other countries?
Has	he / she / it		skied	before?

Short Answers	
Yes, I / you / they / we have.	No, I / you / they / we have not (haven't).
Yes, he / she / it has.	No, he / she / it has not (hasn't).

Exercise

(A) Change the verbs into the correct past participle forms.

> Example   tell ➡ ___told___

1. am / is / are ➡ _____
2. do / does ➡ _____
3. work ➡ _____
4. visit ➡ _____
5. stop ➡ _____
6. come ➡ _____
7. live ➡ _____
8. forget ➡ _____
9. go ➡ _____
10. have ➡ _____
11. make ➡ _____
12. see ➡ _____
13. sing ➡ _____
14. speak ➡ _____
15. spend ➡ _____
16. think ➡ _____
17. play ➡ _____
18. eat ➡ _____
19. try ➡ _____
20. take ➡ _____

(B) Fill in the blanks with the correct present perfect tense forms of the verbs given.

> Example   She (play) ___has played___ poker once.

1. I _____ never (travel) _____ to other countries.

2. I (live) _____ in Germany before.

3. I (have) _____ a broken leg once.

4. _____ you (see) _____ the new movie?

5. _____ he (go) _____ out with Susie before?

6. I (read) _____ *Othello* twice.

7. _____ you (eat) _____ caviar?

8. She _____ never (smoke) _____ before.

(C) Use the words given to make sentences in the present perfect tense.

> Example (Maria / be / to Italy / once) ➡ <u>Maria has been to Italy once.</u>

1. (Ken / not / play golf / before) ➡ _____

2. (I / lose / my wallet / twice) ➡ _____

3. (our team / win / many games) ➡ _____

4. (we / see / that movie / three times) ➡ _____

5. (Tom / study Chinese / before) ➡ _____

6. (Mr. Smith / never / try / Korean food) ➡ _____

7. (I / not / visit / New York / before) ➡ _____

(D) Correct the errors in the sentences.

> Example Tom <u>haven't go</u> snowboarding before.
> hasn't gone

1. I have never be to Italy.

2. I have saw the short film twice.

3. Has Susan and Rick ever been to Guam before?

4. My car has not never break down.

5. My sister have not be drunk before.

6. Have he win the championship?

7. I have take the driving test four times this year.

E Make questions by using the information in the answers.

Questions	Answers
Example Has Peter seen the Pyramids?	No. Peter hasn't seen the Pyramids.

1. _____
   _____?
   Yes. I have driven a convertible car before.

2. _____
   _____?
   No. We haven't watched the new movie.

3. _____
   _____?
   Yes. I have read *The Bible*.

4. _____
   _____?
   No. James hasn't played the guitar before.

5. _____
   _____?
   Yes. They have taken a blood test.

6. _____
   _____?
   No. She hasn't had any part-time jobs before.

PART 2 — How long have you worked here?

Get Started 🎧

18-2. mp3

Read and listen to the dialogue.

Reporter : Your husband, Rick Carlson, is also a famous
lawyer, isn't he?

Gwen : Yes, he is.

Reporter : **How long have you been married** to him?

Gwen : **It has been almost five years.**

Reporter : Did you meet each other at work?

Gwen : Yes, we did.

Reporter : **How long have you worked** for this law firm?

Gwen : **I've worked** here **since** 2002.

Focus

현재완료 시제의 계속적 용법

● 과거의 어떤 시점에서 시작해서 현재 시점까지 계속되고 있는 동작이나 사실을 나타낼 때도 현재완료 시제를 사용합니다. for+기간(period of time), since+시작점(starting point) 과 같은 표현을 문장 내에 동반합니다.

I **have worked** here **for** three years.
나는 3년 동안 여기서 일해오고 있다.
I **have worked** here **since** 2016.
나는 2016년부터 여기서 일해오고 있다.

Mark has been on vacation for two weeks.

I have been a teacher since 2014.

My boyfriend has not (=hasn't) phoned me for three weeks.

Has she been in Paris since 2015? No, she hasn't. She's been there since 2016.

How long have you known Rick? I have (=I've) known him for two years.

> 의문사 'How long'은 의문문 제일 앞에 위치하며, 이는 계속적 용법에서 '얼마나 오랫동안'이라는 의미로 질문을 할 때 사용됩니다. "How long…?"에 대한 답은 위와 같이 기간을 나타내는 for나 since로 대답합니다.

Exercise

(A) Fill in the blanks with *for/since*.

> **Example** Mr. Kim has been our teacher ___for___ two months.

1. Professor Evans has taught at our school _____ 2013.

2. I haven't had a date _____ a long time.

3. We haven't gone to a club _____ last year.

4. Mindy has lived here _____ four years.

5. I have loved chocolates _____ high school.

6. Jack and Jill have been married _____ six months.

(B) Fill in the blanks with the correct present perfect forms of the verbs given.

> **Example** Dave Mason is the mayor of our town. He (be) ___has been___ the mayor since 2010.

1. Steve is a great boxer. He (be) _____ the champion for three years.

2. My family lives in Hawaii. We all (live) _____ here since 2009.

3. Jody has a Ferrari. She (own) _____ that car for three years.

4. Alan has a broken leg. He (stay) _____ in the hospital for a week now.

5. Jane and Steve are friends. They (know) _____ each other for three years.

6. Do you still feel sick? How long _____ you (have) _____ the headache?

7. This company makes refrigerators. It (make) _____ refrigerators for twenty years.

C Use the words given to make questions in the present perfect tense. Then, use *for/since* and the words given to write short answers.

> Example (how long / she / live / in L.A.)　　　　(2015)
>
> ➡ **Q**: ___How long has she lived in L.A.?___　　**A**: ___Since 2015.___

1. (how long / James / know / Erica)　　　　(a year)

   ➡ Q: _____

   _____?　　A: _____

2. (how long / you / play the piano)　　　　(the age of five)

   ➡ Q: _____

   _____?　　A: _____

3. (how long / Ian / be a police officer)　　　　(2013)

   ➡ Q: _____

   _____?　　A: _____

4. (how long / she / work / at a bank)　　　　(two years)

   ➡ Q: _____

   _____?　　A: _____

5. (how long / you / study / English)　　　　(last year)

   ➡ Q: _____

   _____?　　A: _____

6. (how long / Julie / have the flu)　　　　(a week)

   ➡ Q: _____

   _____?　　A: _____

Let's Speak!

Activity-1

A Listen to the conversations and check (✓) if the statements are true or false. 🎧

		True	False
1	• The woman hasn't been to any other countries before.	☐	☐
	• The man has been to Jeju Island many times.	☐	☐
2	• The man hasn't used the Internet these days.	☐	☐
	• The woman has found something strange with the Internet connection.	☐	☐
3	• The woman has lived in Singapore for two years.	☐	☐
	• The man hasn't lived in other countries before.	☐	☐

Activity-2

A With a partner, practice speaking by asking and answering questions in the present perfect tense using the information given.

Julie Kim	be a professional model	about 20 years
Charles and Alice	be married	four years
Samuel Parker	volunteer for charity organization	August 2009
Tasin Shah	participate in bike races	about 20 years
Ben Hant	work for PGD, Inc.	2013
Justin Wong	write news articles	about 10 years

Example **Q**: How long has _____ ?

A: He / She has _____ for / since _____.

Activity-3 Student A

Ⓐ Look at the boxes with question marks. Ask your partner (student B) questions about these people using the present perfect tense and the words given. Then, circle Yes/No with your partner's answers.

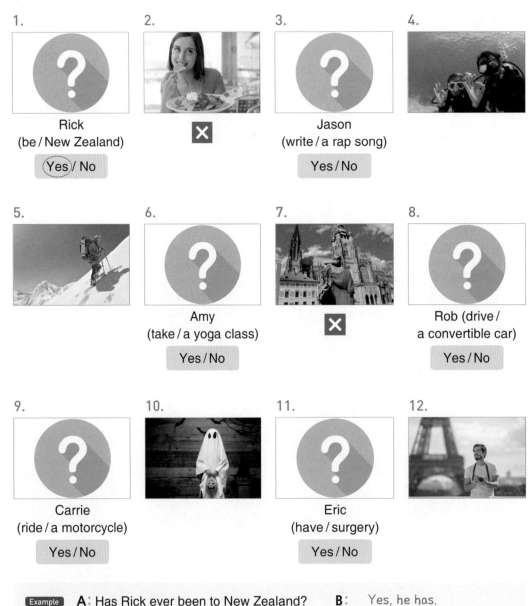

1.
Rick
(be / New Zealand)
Yes / No

2.
✕

3.
Jason
(write / a rap song)
Yes / No

4.

5.

6.
Amy
(take / a yoga class)
Yes / No

7.
✕

8.
Rob (drive /
a convertible car)
Yes / No

9.
Carrie
(ride / a motorcycle)
Yes / No

10.

11.
Eric
(have / surgery)
Yes / No

12.

Example **A:** Has Rick ever been to New Zealand?   **B:** Yes, he has.

Ⓑ Look at the pictures and answer your partner's questions in the present perfect tense. Answer 'No' if an ✕ is marked.

A Look at the boxes with question marks. Ask your partner (student A) questions about these people using the present perfect tense and the words given. Then, circle Yes/No with your partner's answers.

1.

2.
Sally
(eat / Mexican food)
Yes / (No)

3.

4.
John & Richard
(go / scuba diving)
Yes / No

5.
Ken
(climb / Mt. Everest)
Yes / No

6.

7.
Anna (travel
around / Europe)
Yes / No

8.

9.
✕

10.
Mark
(see / a ghost)
Yes / No

11.
✕

12.
Steve
(be / to Paris)
Yes / No

Example **B:** Has Sally ever eaten Mexican food? **A:** No, she hasn't.

B Look at the pictures and answer your partner's questions in the present perfect tense. Answer 'No' if an ✕ is marked.

UNIT 19

Passives

수동태

PART 1 She was born in Boston.

Get Started 🎧

19-1. mp3

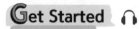

Read and listen to the dialogue.

Sheila Jones is a famous American singer. She **was born** in Boston, on January 3rd, in 1990. Her first album **was recorded** at the age of 20. Her second album **was made** the following year. She **was given** the Best Singer of the Year Award in 2011 for her second album. In October 2015, she **got married** to the famous songwriter, Rick Lee. Over 40 million albums **were sold** worldwide in the year of her marriage.

Focus

▌**수동태** (The passive): **be** 동사＋일반동사의 과거분사형

● 동사의 수동태는 문장에서 행동이나 사건을 일으킨 행위자가 언급되지 않거나 상대적으로 덜 중요하고, 행위 자체에 중점을 두는 경우에 사용됩니다.

1 긍정문: S＋V [be＋과거분사]＋**(by someone)**

	Subject	Verb	Object	
능동태	Jason	**took**	the picture	last week.
수동태	The picture	**was taken**	(by Jason)	last week.

① be 동사의 형태에 주의하세요! 수동태에서 be 동사는 주어의 수나 인칭에 따라 다르며, 시제에 따라서도 그 형태를 바꾸어 주어야 합니다.

	Subject - Singular	Subject - Plural
Present Tense	The picture **is taken** by Jason every day.	The pictures **are taken** by Jason every day.
Past Tense	The picture **was taken** by Jason yesterday.	The pictures **were taken** by Jason yesterday.

② 조동사 (should, can, could 등) 다음에 오는 수동태의 경우, be 동사의 원형인 be가 사용됩니다.

The picture should be taken by Jason.

2 부정문: S+V [be+NOT+과거분사]+(by someone)

능동태	Jason **didn't take** the picture.
수동태	The picture **was not taken** by Jason.

3 의문문

① Yes / No 의문문: 수동태의 평서문 문장에서 be 동사와 주어 자리를 바꾸면 의문문이 됩니다.

The picture was taken last week.	**The pictures were** taken last week.
Was the picture taken last week?	**Were the pictures** taken last week?
- Yes, it was. ❙ - No, it wasn't.	- Yes, they were. ❙ - No, they weren't.

② Wh- 의문문: 의문사를 의문문의 맨 앞에 덧붙입니다.

The picture was taken last week.	**The pictures were** taken last week.
When **was the picture** taken?	When **were the pictures** taken?
- It was taken last week.	- They were taken last week.

Exercise

(A) Fill in the blanks with the correct passive forms of the verbs given.

> **Example** This house (build) _was built_ in 1950.

1. The room (clean) _____ a month ago.

2. The songs (sing) _____ by the singer in 2010.

3. The paintings (paint) _____ by Jackson Pollock.

4. The book (write) _____ by Jane Austin in 1797.

5. Gary's voice (hear) _____ from my office.

6. A lot of sculptures (display) _____ in the museum.

7. The conference (hold) _____ at the Johnson Company last week.

8. Parking (allow) _____ on Main St. last year.

(B) Write the negative forms of the passive sentences in Exercise A.

> **Example** _This house wasn't built in 1950._

1. _____

2. _____

3. _____

4. _____

5. _____

6. _____

7. _____

8. _____

C Complete the passage by using the correct forms of the verbs given.

The Eiffel Tower

Have you heard the Eiffel Tower? Do you know who _____ (design) it? The Eiffel Tower _____ (design) by an engineer Gustave Eiffel and _____ (complete) in 1889. When it _____ (build), it was named the world's tallest structure. However, when the Chrysler Building in New York City _____ (construct) in 1930, the title _____ (lose).

Although it lost its title, it became the symbol of France. Now the Eiffel Tower _____ (visit) by millions of tourists every year.

D Fill in the blanks with the correct passive forms of the verbs given. Use the tenses given.

> **Example** The book (write) _was written_ by James Joyce. [past]

1. The movies (direct) _____ by Steven Spielberg. [past]

2. The rules (need) _____ for any group. [present]

3. The top of the tower (damage) _____ by lightening. [past]

4. The newspaper (pick up) _____ by my dog every morning. [present]

5. The e-mails (send) _____ to the wrong person. [past]

6. English (not speak) _____ in many countries. [present]

7. Two people (hurt) _____ in the car accident. [past]

E Rewrite the sentences in the passive voice.

> **Example** Jeremy picked up the guests yesterday.
>
> ➡ _The guests were picked up by Jeremy yesterday._

1. A thief stole my car yesterday.

   ➡ _____

2. The noise woke the baby up.

   ➡ _____

3. The ball broke the window this morning.

   ➡ _____

4. We can see many old movies on TV.

   ➡ _____

5. The mechanic didn't fix the car.

   ➡ _____

6. A Hungarian newspaper editor invented the ball point pen.

   ➡ _____

7. We didn't make the decision over the weekend.

   ➡ _____

8. Jack doesn't water the plants every day.

   ➡ _____

F Complete the questions and answers using the information given.

> **Example** The information was posted on the Web.
>
> **Q:** _Was_ the _information_ posted on the Web?
> **A:** _Yes, it was._

1. Lunch was served at noon.

   Q: _____ lunch _____ at noon?
   A: No, _____. It was served at 1:00.

2. The cars were made in China.

   Q: _____ the cars _____ in China?

   A: Yes, _____.

3. The schedule was changed right before the meeting.

   Q: _____ the schedule _____ right before the meeting?

   A: Yes, _____.

4. The boxes are delivered every day.

   Q: _____ the boxes _____ every day?

   A: No, _____. They are delivered twice a week.

(G) Complete the questions in the passive voice.

   Example   Two thieves were caught by the police this morning.

      ➡ When (were) the two thieves (caught) by the police?

1. Jenny's car was repaired at the garage yesterday.

   ➡ Where (   ) Jenny's car (   ) yesterday?

2. The special discount is offered at the store every Sunday.

   ➡ When (   ) the special discount (   ) at the store?

3. All flights were canceled because of the heavy fog.

   ➡ Why (   ) all flights (   )?

4. The report was written by Annie last week.

   ➡ When (   ) the report (   ) by Annie?

Let's Speak!

Activity-1

A Compare the two pictures and see what has changed in picture B. Write the changes using the passive voice in the simple past tense and the correct words from the box.

blow	trip	move	damage

1. The leaves _____ by the wind.

2. The trash can _____ to the right.

3. She _____ by the boy.

4. The bench _____ by the bicycle.

B With a partner, practice speaking by talking about the changes in the two pictures.

Activity-2

A Listen to the announcement and check (✓) the items that are mentioned. 🎧

pillows ☐	seatbelts ☐	cellphones ☐
snacks ☐	headsets ☐	carry-on bags ☐
windows ☐	items in the overhead bins ☐	

B Listen to the recording again and write the sentences in the passive voice using the words given. 🎧

> **Example** Seatbelts must (fasten) tightly.
> ➡ Seatbelts must be fastened tightly.

1. Phones should (turn off).

    ➡ _____

2. All the items in the overhead bins should (stow).

    ➡ _____

3. Carry-on bags must (place) under the seats.

    ➡ _____

Activity-3   Student A

A Look at the history of a robot company. It is missing some dates. Ask your partner (student B) about the missing information using the passive voice. Then, fill in the blanks with your partner's answers.

	The company was founded in Portland.
2008	New technology "M" was introduced.
	The company was awarded Technology Company of the Year.
2012	New house robots were made.
	A new factory was built in India.
2017	Over 10,000 robot models were produced.

B Look at the history of the company and answer your partner's questions in the passive voice.

> **Example**   **A**: When was the company founded in Portland?
> **B**: It was founded in 2008.

Activity-3 Student B

(A) Look at the history of a robot company. It is missing some dates. Ask your partner (student A) about the missing information using the passive voice. Then, fill in the blanks with your partner's answers.

2008   The company was founded in Portland.

[   ]   New technology "M" was introduced.

2010   The company was awarded Technology Company of the Year.

[   ]   New house robots were made.

2014   A new factory was built in India.

[   ]   Over 10,000 robot models were produced.

(B) Look at the history of the company and answer your partner's questions in the passive voice.

Example   **B:** When was New technology "M" introduced?
           A: It was introduced in 2008.

UNIT 20

Relative Pronouns
관계대명사

Get Started 🎧

20-1. mp3

Read and listen to the dialogue.

Here is a picture of my family. The person who is on my right is my dad. He works at an accounting company in New York City. The lady who is wearing a dark sweater is my mom. The girl who is standing on my left is my little sister, Jane. She is holding a teddy bear which has a ribbon around its neck.

Focus

관계대명사 (Relative Pronoun) ①

● 관계대명사는 그 앞에 놓인 사람, 동물, 또는 어떤 사물에 대해 부연 설명해주는 절을 이끕니다. 관계대명사절은 크게 주격 관계대명사가 사용된 절과 목적격 관계대명사가 사용된 절로 나누어 볼 수 있습니다.

1 주격 관계대명사(Subject Relative Pronoun): who, that, which

Subject Relative Pronoun		Example
who	사람	I know a girl **who** speaks three languages.
that	사람, 동물, 사물	Greg has a car **that** is 50 years old.
which	동물, 사물	This is the book **which** was written by Greg Miller.

> 관계대명사 that은 who처럼 사람을 대상으로 부연 설명할 때 사용되기도 합니다.
>
> I know the guy **that** speaks three languages.

2 주격 관계대명사절: [선행사+who/which/that+동사]

For People	For Things (or Animals)
I know the guy. + The guy lost his wallet.	I have a picture. + The picture is black and white.
→ I know the guy [**who** lost his wallet].	→ I have a picture [**that (which)** is black and white].
선행사	선행사

> 관계대명사절은 수식하는 어휘(선행사) 바로 뒤에 위치합니다.
>
> 주격 관계대명사 다음의 동사는 선행사가 3인칭 단수인 경우 -(e)s를 붙여 주어야 합니다.
>
> I know the **guy** who **speaks** three languages.
> speak (X)

Exercise

(A) Underline the relative clauses and circle the words that the clauses describe in the sentences.

Example I have a (book) that was published in 1820.

1. Greg is my friend who lives in India.

2. I have a friend who loves rap music.

3. They are the people who work at the office.

4. Paris is the city that is famous for the Eiffel Tower.

5. Kevin lives in a house which has big windows.

6. I know a woman who can speak four languages.

7. My ten-year-old son reads books which are very difficult.

B Circle the correct answers.

> Example I moved the box (who /(which)) weighs 30 kg.

1. Karen drives a car (who / that) is 20 years old.

2. I like to hang out with people (who / which) like wine.

3. Do you know anybody (who / which) has been to Guam?

4. Christina is wearing a red sweater (who / which) looks big on her.

5. Do you know Jeremy (who / which) was in our study group once?

6. Serena always asks me questions (who / which) are easy to answer.

7. What's the name of the man (who / which) is standing next to Linda?

8. An ATM is a machine (who / that) helps us with banking services.

C Rewrite the sentences by using the correct forms of the verbs given.

> Example The new assistant is the woman who (have) long blonde hair.
> ➡ _The new assistant is the woman who has long blonde hair._

1. I met a girl who (live) in the suburbs.

    ➡ _____

2. There was a new book that (have) everything.

    ➡ _____

3. Andy is the man who (be) wearing a black jacket.

    ➡ _____

4. An orange is a kind of fruit that (taste) a bit sour.

    ➡ _____

5. Teachers are the people who (educate) students.

    ➡ _____

6. This is the house that (be) close to the subway station.

→ _____

7. A professional musician is a person who (play) music for a living.

→ _____

8. What's the name of the restaurant that (be) next to the drugstore?

→ _____

(D) Combine the two sentences into one using relative pronouns.

Example   I know a man. He works for the government.
→ I know a man ___who works for the government___ .

1. I saw the old lady. She always wears a red muffler.

→ I saw the old lady _____.

2. Dane caught the boy. He broke the window.

→ Dane caught the boy _____.

3. I am going to the grocery store. It opened yesterday.

→ I am going to the grocery store _____.

4. She fixed the car. It broke down.

→ She fixed the car _____.

5. We met Dr. Tomlin. He is famous for his novels.

→ We met Dr. Tomlin _____.

6. This is the boy. The boy is from Australia.

→ This is the boy _____.

7. Dolphins are clever animals. Dolphins make people happy.

→ Dolphins are clever animals _____.

8. Susie went to the movie theater. The movie theater was built 60 years ago.

→ Susie went to the movie theater _____.

Get Started 🎧

20-2. mp3

Read and listen to the dialogue.

Brian: Has Jody dropped by today?

Leena: Jody? Who is he?

Brian: Oh, come on. He is the one **who** we met at Allen's party last weekend.

Leena: Oh, the tall guy **who** I talked with!

Brian: That's right.

Leena: Why is he coming here today?

Brian: He wants to give us some new ideas about the project **that** we're working on.

Leena: Oh, that's very nice of him.

Focus

▌ 관계대명사 ②

1 목적격 관계대명사(Object Relative Pronoun): who(m), that, which

Object Relative Pronoun		Example
who(m)	사람	He is the person **who(m)** I told you about.
that	사람, 동물, 사물	Greg lives in a house **that** his grandfather built 50 years ago.
which	동물, 사물	This is the book **which** James loves.

> 관계대명사 that은 who(m)처럼 사람을 대상으로 부연 설명할 때 사용되기도 합니다.
> He is the person **that** I told you about.
>
> 기존에는 사람을 가리킬 때 목적격 관계대명사 whom을 사용하기도 했으나, 최근에는 who의 사용이 더 보편화되어 있습니다.

2 목적격 관계대명사절: [선행사 who(m) / which / that+주어+동사]

For People	For Things (or Animals)
I know the guy. + You met the guy yesterday.	I like the cookies. + My mom made the cookies.
→ I know the guy [**who(m)** you met yesterday].	→ I like the cookies [**that (which)** my mom made].
선행사	선행사

3 주격 관계대명사절 vs. 목적격 관계대명사절

주격 관계대명사절	주절 + [who / which / that + 동사 ...]
	This is the book [that / which is written by Octavia Butler.]
목적격 관계대명사절	주절 + [who(m) / which / that + 주어 + 동사 ...]
	This is the book [that / which I read.]

> 주격 관계대명사와는 달리, 목적격 관계대명사는 문장에서 생략될 수 있습니다.
>
> This is the bottle of water I bought this morning.
>
> that / which가 생략됨

Exercise

(A) **Underline the object relative clauses and circle the words that the clauses describe in the sentences.**

> **Example** What did you do with the (box) that I borrowed?

1. I lost the hat that I got yesterday.

2. I ate the apple that my mom bought yesterday.

3. I know the man who Julie is talking to.

4. She liked the tomato soup that I made.

5. That's the book which I told you about yesterday.

6. He is the person who I talked about the other day.

7. Someone borrowed the book that you're looking for.

8. I'm going to visit my grandmother who I miss so much.

B **Combine the two sentences into one using relative pronouns.**

> **Example** There is the black car. I want to buy the car.
> → There is the black car ___that I want to buy___ .

1. Jenny is a student. Everybody likes her.

   → Jenny is a student _____ .

2. There are some fashion magazines. Jessica likes those fashion magazines.

   → There are some fashion magazines _____ .

3. My sister is holding a new bag. I bought the bag yesterday.

   → My sister is holding a new bag _____ .

4. Summer is the season. I like summer the best.

   → Summer is the season _____ .

5. Where are the dogs? I need to take care of the dogs for Linda.

   → Where are the dogs _____ ?

6. That's the toy. My daughter likes to play with the toy.

   → That's the toy _____ .

7. She wore a mask. She got the mask for the costume party.

   → She wore a mask _____ .

8. This is my older brother. You met him a month ago.

   → This is my older brother _____ .

C Circle the relative pronouns in the sentences and check (√) whether they are subject pronouns or object pronouns.

	Subject Pronoun	Object Pronoun
Example It was an excellent idea (that) Mr. Kim presented.		√
1. I lost the pen that you lent me.		
2. Penguins are animals that live in cold places.		
3. I'm going to stay at the hotel which Susan talked about.		
4. My brother is the person who won the boxing match.		
5. I know a woman who has seven sisters.		
6. That's the book which I liked the best.		
7. It was the best movie that I've ever seen.		
8. Do you know the man who got married last month?		

D Check (√) the sentences with relative pronouns that can be omitted.

1. The movie that I watched last night was fantastic. (　　　)

2. The woman who we met at the party is going to get married soon. (　　　)

3. Do you know the name of the Thai restaurant that is near the department store? (　　　)

4. The man who Sally is talking to is my roommate. (　　　)

5. I bought a house which has four bedrooms. (　　　)

6. A violin is a musical instrument that has four strings. (　　　)

Let's Speak!

Activity-1

(A) With a partner, practice speaking by asking and answering question using relative clauses and the words given. Make sure to use the correct relative pronouns and the correct forms of the verbs given.

> **Example**   writer, (write), *Romeo and Juliet*/ Shakespeare
> **A**: What's the name of the ___writer who wrote *Romeo and Juliet*___?
> **B**: ___The writer who wrote *Romeo and Juliet* is Shakespeare.___

1. author, (write), *Harry Potter*/ J.K. Rowling

2. pub, (be), near the shoe shop / Cheers

3. group, (sing), *Let It Be*/ The Beatles

4. river, (flow through) Paris / Seine

5. movie director, (direct) *E.T.*/ Steven Spielberg

Activity-2

(A) Listen to the recording and check (✓) the person who is being described. 🎧

Danielle Norris ☐

Ashley Janes ☐

Cindy Knowles ☐

B Listen to the recording again and fill in the blanks. 🎧

- famous TV talk show host

- lives in _____

- _____ woman to anchor a major _____

- _____ her own _____ company

- has produced several _____

Activity-3

A With a partner, practice speaking by using relative clauses to describe the items in the box to each other. Try to guess what your partner is describing.

watermelon   cup   chair

laptop   air-conditioner   stapler

Example   This is something that you can eat.

Answer Keys

UNIT 01 **Simple Present of *Be* verb**
Be동사의 현재시제

PART **1**

(A) 1. am   2. are   3. is   4. are
    5. is   6. is   7. are   8. is

(B) 1. I'm not in bed.
    2. Both movies aren't popular.
    3. The capital of Australia isn't Sydney.
    4. You and I aren't from Italy.
    5. My cats aren't on the couch.
    6. Grant isn't a voice actor.
    7. They aren't in line. / They're not in line.
    8. It isn't cold outside. / It's not cold outside.

(C) 1. We are from Canada.
    2. I am not a student.
    3. The classrooms aren't big.
    4. It is not a ball.
    5. They are not in love.
    6. Freddy and Fiona are best friends.
    7. Julia and David are a couple.
    8. Jack is not diligent.

(D) 1. **Mark :**   How <u>are</u> you today, Melissa?
    Melissa : I <u>am</u> fine. How about you?
    Mark :   I <u>am</u> so worried. The final exams
             <u>are</u> next week.
    Melissa : That's true. But I <u>am not</u> worried.
    Mark :   Why not?
    Melissa: Because I <u>am</u> in a study group now.

2. **Kristin:** Hi, my name <u>is</u> Kristin. I <u>am</u> a new
            student.
   Scott: Nice to meet you, Kristin. I <u>am</u> Scott.
   Kristin: Scott, what's your major?
   Scott: My major <u>is</u> Biology.
   Kristin: Wow, same here. How are the classes?
   Scott: All the classes <u>are</u> great, except
            Professor Smith's class.
   Kristin: Why is that?
   Scott: Because his lecture <u>is</u> so boring.

(E) 1. My dog is not / isn't very cute.
    2. We are not / We aren't / We're not good at
       speaking English.
    3. My older sister is not / isn't a nurse.
    4. All the office workers are not / aren't from
       different countries.
    5. My mom and dad are not / aren't in the
       Philippines.
    6. Bottles of water are not / aren't in the
       refrigerator.
    7. That song is not / isn't popular all over the
       world.
    8. I am not / I'm not in charge of hiring new
       employees.

PART **2**

(A) 1. d   2. c   3. f   4. a
    5. b   6. g   7. e

(B) 1. **Q:** Are the textbooks expensive?
       A: Yes, they are.

2. **Q:** Am I on time?
   A: No, you aren't. You are late.

3. Q: Is this book yours?
   A: No, it isn't. It's my brother's.

4. Q: Is German your native language? / Is your native language German?
   A: Yes, it is.

5. Q: Is your best friend from Korea?
   A: Yes, he/she is.

6. Q: Are you and I on the same team?
   A: No, we aren't. We are on different teams.

(C) 1. A: Are they new sunglasses?
   B: Yes, they are. I got them in a duty-free store.
   A: They are very nice and fancy.
   B: Thanks. Is your coat made of real fur?
   A: Hmm... no, it isn't. It is an imitation.
   B: Oh, really? It looks like real fur.

2. A: Is the capital of Korea Busan?
   B: No, it isn't. The capital of Korea is Seoul.
   A: Let's see... How about Italy? Is the capital of Italy Rome?
   B: Yes, it is. People sometimes think it is Milano, but it isn't.

3. A: Are you new here?
   B: Yes, I am.
   A: Oh, welcome to Sunnydale dormitory.
   B: Thanks. Are you happy here?
   A: Yes, I am. Everybody here is very friendly and nice.
   B: That is nice. Are the campus buildings near here?
   A: Yes, they are.
   B: How about the gym? Is it nearby?
   A: Of course. It is right across the street.

PART 3

(A) 1. Who's in the kitchen?
   a. Mr. Kim is in the kitchen.

2. When is your class over?
   b. My class is over soon.

3. Where is the wedding?
   a. The wedding is at the church.

4. Where are you from?
   c. I am from Belgium.

5. How is your new job?
   a. My new job is great.

6. What time is it?
   b. It's 3 o'clock.

7. What color is your bag?
   c. My bag is silver. / It's silver. / The color of my bag is silver.

(B) 1. Q: What are(→ is) the name of the new guy?
   A: His name're(→ is) Kevin.

2. Q: Who(→ When) is Christmas?
   A: It am(→ is / 's) on December 25th.

3. Q: How are(→ is) the weather?
   A: It are(→ is / 's) cold and windy.

4. Q: When're(→ is / 's) the Labor Day in the U.S.?
   A: They're(→ It is / It's) in September.

5. Q: How much is(→ are) these earrings?
   A: It's(→ They are / They're) $10.

6. Q: What time are(→ is) the flight?
   A: It are(→ is / 's) 8 pm.

7. Q: How are(→ is) the movie?
   A: It're(→ is / 's) OK.

(C) 1. Tom: Sorry. Am I late for this party?
   Amber: Don't worry. You are on time.
   Tom: Oh, good.
   Amber: Come on in.
   Tom: Amber, who is the person over there?
   Amber: She is my neighbor, Hanna.

Tom: How old is she?

Amber: She's 24. Are you interested in her?

Tom: Yes, I am.

2. **Jeff:** Hello? Who is this?

Fiona: This is Fiona. Is Jeff there?

Jeff: Speaking.

Fiona: Hi, Jeff. How are you today?

Jeff: I am fine. So, what's up?

Fiona: I want to ask you about your English class. Is the class easy?

Jeff: No, it isn't. I think it's really hard for beginners.

Fiona: Oh, I see. Who is the teacher?

Jeff: The teacher is Rick Newton.

Fiona: Where is he from?

Jeff: He is from England.

Fiona: Oh, I see.

3. **Ian:** What is your name?

Carol: My name is Carol. Nice to meet you.

Ian: Nice to meet you, too. I am Ian. Do you live near here?

Carol: Yes. By the way, what time is it now?

Ian: Oh, it is 7:40. I hope the bus comes soon.

Carol: I hope so, too. How far is it to downtown?

Ian: It's only three stops away.

4. **Nicole:** Wow! What a lovely picture! Are they your family?

Mr. Kim: Yes, they are.

Nicole: Who is she next to you?

Mr. Kim: She's my wife, Helen. She is lovely.

Nicole: And are they your children?

Mr. Kim: Yes, they are.

Nicole: How old are they?

Mr. Kim: Philip is seven and Sue is four years old.

Nicole: They are so cute.

UNIT 02

Pronouns
대명사

PART 1

Ⓐ 1. she 2. they 3. they 4. he
5. they 6. it 7. they 8. you
9. we 10. they 11. it 12. they
13. she 14. we

Ⓑ 1. It will be fun!
2. They are in England now.
3. We like jogging together.
4. They help me with my homework.
5. It is also a famous tourist spot.
6. Now, he doesn't have it.
7. Sally and I already had breakfast because we got up early.

Ⓒ 1. Ms. Gellar loves them.
2. Jane wants to sell it.
3. The officer talked to us.
4. Sally sent e-mails to them.
5. I'll put them on the wall.
6. He took her to a fancy restaurant.

Ⓓ 1. They all like her.
2. He will give them to Jen.
3. So, she doesn't talk to them often.
4. She wants to throw them away.
5. He really wants to meet them.
6. They are very nice to us.
7. He got it for his birthday.

Ⓔ Mr. Simpson and Mrs. Simpson got married 15 years ago. Them(→ They) have two beautiful children, Joanna and Peter. They try to spend more time with they(→ them). Joanna is 12 years old. Her(→ She) just entered middle school. Her(→ She) is always at the top of the class, and everybody likes she(→ her). She has lots of good friends. She sometimes invites they(→ them) to her home and plays games together. Peter is six years old. He goes to kindergarten. He can't go to school by himself, so Mrs. Simpson takes he(→ him) there every morning. Him(→ He) loves singing and dancing in front of his family and friends.

PART 2

(A) 1. Fred is happy with his job.

2. That's Tom's motorcycle.

3. Mr. and Mrs. Jones are not living with their children now.

4. I forgot to bring my umbrella today. Can I borrow one of yours?

5. You went over the speed limit. Can I see your driver's license?

6. My wife and I are going to buy our own house next year.

7. The students' grades are emailed to their parents.

8. Ms. Berry is Tom and Chris's private tutor.

(B) 1. This is Susan's cat. That's yours.

2. The best students in our school are Mr. Kelly's.

3. That is Cathy's phone. I'm sure it's hers.

4. These sketchbooks aren't mine. They're my children's.

5. Robin parks his car in this parking lot. The red car is his.

6. Sally's boyfriend bought her a necklace. That necklace is hers.

7. Today is our 2nd wedding anniversary. We will have dinner at my friend's restaurant.

8. That's not my car. That's my brother's. Mine is over there.

(C) 1. Are those yours?

2. I did't have an umbrella, so Mina lent me hers.

3. The black one is his.

4. That isn't ours.

5. Is it yours?

6. The robots are my children's.

7. Did you buy the paintings at Claire's?

8. It's their fault, not ours.

(D) 1. This table is (our / ours).

2. Fiona likes (hers / her) roommate.

3. It's none of (yours / your) business.

4. We hope for (their / theirs) happiness.

5. The elephant moves (it's / its) nose slowly.

6. The (boys' / boys's) tennis match is tomorrow.

7. They went to the movies with (their / theirs) co-workers.

8. (Sam and Sally's / Sam's and Sally's) wedding is on September 3rd.

PART 3

(A)-1 1. this   2. these   3. this   4. these
      5. this   6. these

(A)-2 1. that   2. those   3. that   4. those
      5. that   6. those

(B) 1. Those are rabbits under the table.

2. That is a nice wedding dress.

3. This letter is for you.

4. Those are nice restaurants.

5. These red umbrellas are Jane's.

6. This is from China.

7. That apple is not for eating.

(C) 1. No, it isn't. This is a squirrel.

2. No, it isn't. That is my toothbrush.

3. No, they're not. Those are my pants.

4. No, they're not. These are my earrings.

5. No, it isn't. This is mine.

6. No, they aren't. Those are my sister's.

(D) 1. Whose books are those?

They are Daniel's.

2. Whose cellphones are these?

They are Tom's.

3. Whose flower vase is this?

It is Daisy's.

4. Whose laptop is that?

It is Rob's.

5. Whose clock is that?

It is Jade's.

6. Whose picture frame is this?

It is Fred's.

PART 4

(A) 1. d   2. f   3. b   4. a

5. c   6. e

(B) 1. **Q:** What time is it now?

A: It's three thirty.

2. **Q:** What date is it today?

A: It's May 8th.

3. **Q:** What day is it today?

A: It's Wednesday.

4. **Q:** How far is it to the City Hall?

A: It's a ten-minute walk from here.

(C) 1. I   2. O   3. I   4. O

5. S   6. I   7. S   8. I

9. O   10. I

UNIT 03   Simple Present
현재시제

PART 1

(A)-1

1. The dog <u>swims</u> in the lake.

2. She <u>dresses</u> all in pink for parties.

3. Scott always <u>works</u> in his office until 9 pm.

4. Sally always <u>finishes</u> her paper on time.

5. My cousin <u>draws</u> pictures very well.

6. Allison <u>sleeps</u> in on Sunday mornings.

7. My younger brother sometimes <u>plays</u> soccer with his friends.

(A)-2

1. [s] ⟨z⟩ [ɪz]   2. [s] [z] ⟨ɪz⟩

3. ⟨s⟩ [z] [ɪz]   4. [s] [z] ⟨ɪz⟩

5. [s] ⟨z⟩ [ɪz]   6. ⟨s⟩ [z] [ɪz]

7. [s] ⟨z⟩ [ɪz]

(B) 1. do → does   2. have → has

3. carrys → carries   4. bark → barks

5. goes → go   6. don't → doesn't

7. do → does, plays → play, love → loves

(C) 1. He <u>doesn't pay</u> the rent every month.

2. We <u>don't have</u> enough money for a party.

3. The bird <u>doesn't fly</u> high up in the sky.

4. The children <u>don't watch</u> TV these days.

5. Freddy <u>doesn't do</u> his homework sometimes.

6. Jane <u>doesn't wash</u> her hair in the morning.

(D) I <u>live</u> with my roommate. His name is Ken. He is a night owl, but I am an early bird. I usually <u>go</u> to bed before midnight and <u>wake up</u> at 6 am. However, Ken <u>goes</u> to bed around 2 or 3 in the morning. He sometimes <u>parties</u> until 6 am. Then he <u>comes</u> back home and <u>sleeps</u>. All my classes <u>start</u> early, but Ken always <u>goes</u> to school after lunch. We don't <u>have</u> anything in common, but we <u>get</u> along well.

PART 2

(A) 1. **Q:** <u>Does</u> your sister <u>clean her room</u> every day?

   A: Yes, <u>she does.</u>

2. **Q:** <u>Does</u> he <u>exercise</u> a lot?

   A: No, <u>he doesn't.</u>

3. **Q:** <u>Do</u> they <u>argue</u> often?

   A: Yes, <u>they do.</u>

4. **Q:** <u>Does</u> she <u>read</u> a lot?

   A: No, <u>she doesn't.</u>

5. **Q:** <u>Does</u> she <u>eat meat</u>?

   A: No, <u>she doesn't.</u>

(B) 1. Does Alex always sleep late? No, he doesn't.

2. Does Sarah wash her clothes on Saturdays? Yes, she does.

3. Does your baby cry all night? No, he/she doesn't.

4. Does your sister help you with your homework? Yes, she does.

5. Do you need the car today? No, I don't.

6. Do they go to the movies every weekend? Yes, they do.

PART 3

(A) 1. d   2. f   3. h   4. b
   5. a   6. g   7. c   8. e

(B) 1. How does the laptop work? It works well.

2. Where does Freddy work? At the post office.

3. When do I start my job? Next month.

4. What does your sister do? She is a student.

5. Why does he like the book? Because it's very interesting.

6. What do you do on weekends? I usually go hiking.

(C) **Interviewer:** <u>Where do you live?</u>

Interviewee: I live in Granville.

Interviewer: <u>Who do you</u> live with?

Interviewee: I live with my parents and brother.

Interviewer: Where <u>do your parents work</u>?

Interviewee: My father works at a bank, and my mother works at an elementary school.

Interviewer: <u>What does your brother</u> do?

Interviewee: My brother is a reporter.

Interviewer: Why <u>do you</u> want to work for this company?

Interviewee: Because I can learn many things about magazines.

UNIT 04

Nouns & Articles
명사와 관사

PART 1

(A) 1. a   2. an   3. an   4. a
   5. a   6. an   7. an   8. a
   9. an   10. a   11. a   12. a
   13. an 14. a

(B) 1. a   2. a   3. a   4. an
   5. an   6. an   7. a   8. an

(C) 1. boxes   2. animal   3. lily
   4. stories   5. pianos   6. fish
   7. mice   8. photos   9. tooth
   10. roofs   11. children 12. sheep

(D) 1. We bought umbrellas.

2. Apples fall from trees.

3. There are books on the tables.

4. I bought peaches and bananas.

5. Cats are good pets.

6. Photographers take photos.

7. There are elephants in the zoos.

PART 2

(A)

Count Nouns	Non-Count Nouns
apple	furniture
telephone	money
vegetable	rice
flower	information
tooth	bread
girl	knowledge
computer	traffic
pencil	food
book	coffee
T-shirt	advice
dollar	air
word	happiness

(B) 1. b or g   2. d   3. e   4. a
5. f   6. c   7. h   8. i
9. g or b

(C) 1. I have many furnitures(→ much furniture / many pieces of furniture) in my room.

2. Could you give me some advices(→ advice)?

3. He needs an information(→ some information) about the event.

4. I am so tired. I really need some coffees(→ coffee).

5. I don't have many hairs(→ much hair).

6. She usually eats two bowl(→ bowls) of rices(→ rice).

7. She majors in an Economics.

8. Can I have two loaf(→ loaves) of bread, please?

PART 3

(A) Tim thinks a dog is a lovely pet. He loves dogs. He adopted a puppy yesterday. He has three puppies at home. Tim feeds the puppies three times a day.

Every Friday is a special day for the puppies. Tim usually gives them a bath. The puppy with white fur runs away every time before the bath time. After the bath, he takes them to the park.

(B) 1. a   2. a   3. a   4. a
5. a   6. a   7. An, a   8. The

(C) 1. **Helen:** Tony, here is a package for you.
   Tony: Really? Who is it from?
   Helen: I'm not sure, but it says the package is from Belgium.
   Tony: Belgium? Oh, then that's from my uncle. He owns a chocolate shop in Belgium.

2. **Cory:** What do you want to do today?
   Emily: I want to see a movie.
   Cory: What movie do you want to watch?
   Emily: The one with the superheroes. I don't know the title of this movie.
   Cory: Oh, you mean *Ultra Force*? Where do you want to see the film?
   Emily: I know a movie theater downtown. It has a huge screen and a good sound system. The theater is called Max.
   Cory: Okay. I'll reserve the tickets.

PART 4

(A) 1. There aren't (some, (any)) hospitals near my house.

2. Is there (some, (any)) homework for tomorrow?

3. There is ((some), any) orange juice in the fridge.

4. I ate ((some), any) apples for a snack.

5. Do you read (some, (any)) of Shakespeare's dramas?

6. I didn't have (some, (any)) time, so I couldn't go to her party.

7. Did you write (some, (any)) essays in English?

(B) 1. many   2. much   3. many   4. much

5. much

(C) 1. Is there some(→ any) jam in the refrigerator?

2. There are much(→ many) bananas.

3. I invited much(→ many) friends to my birthday party.

4. I'm so full. I ate too many(→ much) bread.

5. I'm writing a paper. I need many(→ much) information.

UNIT 05 Present Progressive
현재진행시제

PART 1

(A) 1. feeling   2. taking   3. stopping

4. planning   5. raining   6. fixing

7. coming   8. sleeping   9. carrying

10. shining   11. thinking   12. tanning

13. watching   14. smiling   15. waiting

16. agreeing   17. using   18. preferring

19. playing   20. paying

(B) 1. The Sun is shining.

2. Tom and Jane are studying in the library.

3. People are watching a movie in the cinema.

4. Fiona is running on the ground.

5. He is polishing his shoes.

6. The man is wearing a sweater.

7. They are shaking hands.

(C) 1. She is not riding her bicycle.

2. Victoria is not having lunch with friends.

3. She is not waiting for the bus now.

4. The students are not playing soccer.

5. Susan and I are not swimming in the pool.

6. They are not talking on the phone right now.

7. James is not carrying his suitcase on the plane.

(D) Today is Monday. It is 8:30 in the morning. People are already at work. Some people are making coffee and some people are eating breakfast in the cafeteria. In the office, I am reading a newspaper. Some people are checking their e-mails. The manager is talking to her assistant. Peter is carrying some copies of a report. Ryan is talking on the phone. Jesse is working at her computer. Tony and Susie are having a meeting. Everyone is getting ready for the first day of the week. I hope this week goes well.

PART 2

(A) 1. Q: Is John having lunch with Stacy?
   A: Yes, he is.

2. Q: Are they working in the office?
   A: No, they aren't.

3. Q: Am I talking too fast?
   A: No, you're not.

4. Q: Is he wearing a blue sweater?
   A: Yes, he is.

5. Q: Are you guys studying for the exam?
   A: Yes, we are.

6. Q: Is she making dinner now?
   A: No, she isn't.

7. Q: Are you taking the yoga class?
   A: Yes, I am. / Yes, we are.

8. Q: Are you seeing anyone?
   A: Yes, I am.

9. **Q:** Is she taking pictures of her children?

   A: No, she isn't.

10. **Q:** Are they waiting for their turn?

    A: Yes, they are.

B 1. Are Gary and Eric playing golf?

   No, they aren't. They are playing football.

2. Are they looking for their car?

   No, they aren't. They are looking for their bicycle.

3. Is the manager going over the report?

   Yes, he/she is.

4. Is Ms. Lee doing the laundry?

   Yes, she is.

5. Is the boss coming now?

   No, he/she isn't. He/She is in his/her office now.

6. Is he taking a walk in the park?

   No, he isn't. He is watching TV at home.

7. Is the baby looking at the baby mobile?

   Yes, he/she is.

8. Is she wearing a black suit?

   Yes, she is.

9. Are you writing a letter?

   Yes, I am. / Yes, we are.

10. Are they talking about me?

    No, they're not. They are talking about somebody else.

PART 3

A 1. Where is she sitting?

   (a) She is sitting at the front row.

2. What are you doing?

   (c) I'm cleaning the room.

3. How are you and Gary doing these days?

   (b) We are doing fine.

4. Why is he yawning?

   (a) Because he is feeling tired.

5. Who are they having dinner with?

   (b) They are having dinner with their classmates.

6. What is he fixing?

   (c) He is fixing a motorcycle.

7. Where are the people singing now?

   (a) They are singing on the street.

B 1. How are(→ is) he doing?

   - He are(→ is) doing well.

2. When(→ What) is she playing with?

   - She's playing with her toy.

3. Why are you read (→ reading) this book?

   - Because I'm studying this author.

4. What(→ Who) are they playing tennis with?

   - They're playing tennis with Jason.

5. What is Sally do(→ doing) now?

   - She studies(→ is studying) for the exam.

C 1. **Ian:** Where are you going now?

   Lisa: I'm going to the supermarket. How about you?

   Ian: I'm waiting for Chris. He's on his way here now.

2. **Travis:** Hey, what are you doing?

   Stacey: I'm chatting online.

   Travis: Who are you talking to?

   Stacey: Brian.

3. **Lisa:** Hello.

   Austin: Hello. This is Austin. What are you doing?

   Lisa: Oh, hi! I'm just watching TV at home.

   Austin: How is the weather in New Jersey?

   Lily: Hmm... It's snowing. My kids are making snowmen and having a snowball fight.

   Austin: Oh, I see. How are you feeling these days?

   Lily: I'm feeling better. I'm exercising these days.

   Austin: Good. Take care. I'll call you later. Bye.

UNIT 06 — Simple Past of *Be* verb
Be 동사의 과거시제

PART 1

Ⓐ 1. was   2. was   3. were   4. were
5. were   6. was   7. was   8. were

Ⓑ 1. Jane wasn't at school yesterday.
2. It wasn't sunny this morning.
3. This backpack wasn't expensive.
4. Danny and Sarah weren't in Paris a few months ago.
5. They weren't at work last Friday.
6. Travis wasn't at the movies with Gina last night.

Ⓒ 1. I was nervous during the speech.
2. They were on vacation in Fiji.
3. Sue wasn't mad at her brother this morning.
4. The shoes were not expensive.
5. People were very excited at the concert.
6. The food wasn't good at the buffet.

Ⓓ 1. was, is   2. was, am   3. were, are
4. were   5. is, was   6. was, is
7. weren't, were   8. were, were

PART 2

Ⓐ 1. Were, wasn't   2. Was, was
3. When, was   4. Where, were
5. How, was   6. Were, were
7. What, was   8. Who, was

Ⓑ 1. Was, c, was   2. Was, d, wasn't
3. Was, a, were   4. Were, g, were

5. were, b, was   6. When, h, was
7. How, f, was   8. What, e, was

Ⓒ 1. **Jamie:** Hey, I called you several times last week, but you weren't home. Where were you?
Mindy: Oh, I was at my grandmother's. She was sick, so I took care of her. Anyway, why did you call me?
Jamie: Actually, I had my birthday party last week.
Mindy: Really? When was your birthday?
Jamie: It was last Friday. Many people were at the party.
Mindy: Oh, I'm sorry that I couldn't make it.

2. **Stephen:** Monica, how was the concert last night?
Monica: It was OK. I enjoyed it, but the music was so loud.
Stephen: Was it crowded with many people?
Monica: Yeah, Many people were there.
Stephen: Were Pete and Kelly there, too?
Monica: No, they weren't. They were at work.
Stephen: What time was the concert?
Monica: It started at 7:30 pm.
Stephen: Where was it?
Monica: It was at the Civic Art Center.

3. **Sue:** Were you and Ben at the meeting?
Fred: No, we weren't.
Sue: Then where were you guys?
Fred: We were with our clients at the restaurant. Actually, we didn't know about the meeting. When was it?
Sue: It was at 1:30. The information was on the bulletin board.
Fred: Oh, we didn't check it. What was it about?
Sue: It was about sales reports.

UNIT 07 — Simple Past
과거시제

PART 1

(A)
1. did
2. helped
3. brought
4. stopped
5. drank
6. thought
7. played
8. bought
9. arrived
10. studied
11. went
12. had
13. carried
14. opened
15. found
16. made
17. showed
18. drove
19. stood
20. forgot

(B)
1. watched
2. did
3. went
4. ate
5. fell
6. met
7. finished
8. practiced

(C)
1. I didn't finish my report yesterday.
2. We didn't enjoy our vacation in Fiji.
3. I didn't go to the gym yesterday.
4. They didn't eat hamburgers for lunch.
5. Julia didn't come to my house yesterday.
6. Carrie didn't write an email to her friend.
7. She didn't take her car to the garage.

(D)
1. made
2. studied
3. didn't watch, watched
4. ran
5. called
6. didn't ride, rode
7. didn't drink, drank

(E) I <u>had</u> a really busy day today! In the morning, I <u>prepared</u> a presentation for a business conference. Then I <u>met</u> my friends during lunch time. We <u>chatted</u> for an hour. After I <u>came</u> back to the office, I <u>made</u> my presentation. A lot of people were there. I was nervous, but I <u>finished</u> the presentation successfully. Later in the afternoon, my co-workers and I <u>went</u> to a bar for some beer.

PART 2

(A)
1. **Q:** Did they go to the wedding?
   A: Yes, they did.

2. **Q:** Did you find the wallet?
   A: No, I didn't.

3. **Q:** Did she get off from work?
   A: Yes, she did.

4. **Q:** Did all of them travel to Europe?
   A: No, they didn't.

5. **Q:** Did she work all day yesterday?
   A: Yes, she did.

6. **Q:** Did you enjoy the movie?
   A: Yes, I did.

7. **Q:** Did Sarah stay home?
   A: No, she didn't.

(B)
1. Did they <u>go</u> home early last night?
2. <u>Did</u> she make pancakes last weekend?
3. Did you <u>arrive</u> in New York this morning?
4. <u>Did</u> Ron and Darren <u>hand</u> in their papers?
5. <u>Did</u> your family move to the U.S. in 2015?
6. <u>Did</u> they <u>stay</u> late at the office yesterday?

(C)
1. **Q:** Did she finally find a better job?
   A: Yes, she did.

2. **Q:** Did he and his friends catch the flu at the same time?
   A: Yes, they did.

3. **Q:** Did Mary get a birthday present from her husband?
   A: Yes, she did.

4. **Q:** Did Sasha and Mario get home early last night?
   A: No, they didn't.

5. **Q:** Did Chandler take his family to the resort last weekend?

   A: No, he didn't.

6. **Q:** Did they have lunch with the president?

   A: No, they didn't.

7. **Q:** Did your co-workers help you a lot with the project?

   A: Yes, they did.

(D) 1. **Jane:** Katie, <u>did</u> you <u>meet</u> Jerry last night?

   Katie: No, I <u>didn't</u>. My boss <u>gave</u> me a lot of work yesterday, so I <u>stayed</u> late at the office.

   Jane: Oh, that's a shame.

2. **Melissa:** <u>Did</u> you <u>have</u> a nice weekend?

   James: Yes, I did. I <u>went</u> to see a musical.

   Melissa: Wow, how was it?

   James: It was fantastic! I really <u>loved</u> it.

3. **Ashley:** <u>Did</u> you <u>call</u> me last night?

   Brian: Yes, I <u>did</u>, but you <u>didn't answer</u> the phone.

   Ashley: I <u>was</u> at our company dinner.

   Brian: What did you have?

   Ashley: I <u>had</u> Chinese food.

   Brian: Oh, I see. <u>Did</u> you <u>have</u> a good time?

   Ashley: Yes, I <u>did</u>.

PART 3

(A) 1. (What) (did) you (buy) from the grocery store?

2. (When) (did) he (call) me?

3. (Who) (did) they (sit) with?

4. (Where) (did) she (live) before?

5. (How) (did) you (go) there?

6. (Why) (did) the manager (yell) at you?

7. (When) (did) Tim (come) back?

8. (What) (did) you guys (talk) about?

(B) 1. **A:** What <u>did you eat</u> for dessert?

   B: I ate frozen yogurt.

   A: How <u>did it taste</u>?

   B: It tasted great.

2. **A:** Did you call me yesterday?

   B: Yes, I did.

   A: What time <u>did you call me</u>?

   B: I <u>called</u> you at 10.

3. **A:** How much <u>did you pay</u> for the jacket?

   B: I paid 600 dollars for it.

   A: Where <u>did you buy it</u>?

   B: I bought it at Daisy's.

4. **A:** Where <u>did you go</u> with your girlfriend yesterday?

   B: We went to the movies yesterday.

   A: What movie <u>did you watch</u>?

   B: We watched a horror movie.

5. **A:** How was your holiday?

   B: It was relaxing.

   A: What <u>did you do</u>?

   B: I just stayed home and baked.

   A: What <u>did you bake</u>?

   B: I baked some cookies and bread.

(C) 1. <u>What</u> color suits <u>did they wear</u>?

2. <u>What did he buy</u> you for your birthday?

3. <u>Why did she cry</u>?

4. <u>When did the delivery arrive</u>?

5. <u>Where did you pick up</u> your mom?

6. <u>How did you get</u> here?

UNIT 08 Past Progressive
과거진행시제

PART 1

(A)
1. <u>Erin was shopping online</u> yesterday.
2. <u>It was raining</u> yesterday.
3. <u>Andy was working out</u> at the gym <u>yesterday</u>.
4. <u>He was giving a presentation yesterday</u>.
5. <u>Many people were watching a concert yesterday</u>.
6. <u>I was working hard</u> in the office <u>yesterday</u>.
7. <u>We were taking a walk</u> in the park <u>yesterday</u>.

(B)
1. Carrie and Sean weren't having coffee together at 4 pm.
2. Freddie and I weren't hiking the mountain when my phone rang.
3. Steve wasn't reading a newspaper when he heard a siren.
4. We weren't waiting in line when we saw a pickpocket.
5. They weren't having a discussion at that time.
6. He wasn't working on the computer when he heard a strange sound.
7. I wasn't doing the dishes while my husband was cleaning the floor.
8. My roommate wasn't listening to music while I was cooking dinner.

(C)
1. was jogging / began
2. was doing / rang
3. was delivering / barked
4. was gambling / was travelling
5. was walking / went

(D) were moving / were working on / was looking for / was looking at / was shouting at

PART 2

(A)
1. **Q:** Were Sam and David talking loudly when the teacher came in?
   A: Yes, they were.

2. **Q:** Was Ryan sleeping at midnight last night?
   A: No, he wasn't.

3. **Q:** Was she studying abroad when her nephew was born?
   A: Yes, she was.

4. **Q:** Were you having a weekly meeting when the phone rang?
   A: Yes, we were.

5. **Q:** Were you paying attention during the class?
   A: No, I wasn't.

6. **Q:** Were they shopping while you were playing basketball?
   A: Yes, they were.

7. **Q:** Was he working at the office when a burglar broke in?
   A: Yes, he was.

(B)
1. (d) was working
2. Was it snowing / (a)
3. Was Cindy reading / (f) wasn't
4. was Mark running / (c)
5. Were Peter and Dan sleeping / (b) were
6. were you hiding / (g)
7. Was he talking on the phone / (e) wasn't

(C)
1. Where were you waiting for me yesterday?
   I was waiting for you in the library.

2. What was he doing during the class?
   He was talking on the phone.

3. Who were you calling when I entered the room?
   I was calling a repairman.

4. What was Tom buying when the policeman came?

   He was buying a pack of cigarettes.

5. Why was she running while he was walking?

   Because she was late for class.

6. Where were they going when we saw them?

   They were going to the supermarket.

UNIT 09 — Questions
의문문

PART 1

(A) 1. i 2. c 3. d 4. a 5. b
6. h 7. g 8. j 9. f 10. e

(B) 1. Q: Who likes horror movies?
   A: My younger brother likes horror movies.

2. Q: Who speaks French well?
   A: Brian speaks French well.

3. Q: Who wore pink pants to work?
   A: Cindy wore pink pants to work.

4. Q: Who is behind the door?
   A: My daughter is behind the door.

5. Q: Who was angry at Carol?
   A: Michael was angry at Carol.

6. Q: What makes Thomas busy?
   A: His work makes him busy.

7. Q: What is burning in the kitchen?
   A: The dinner is burning in the kitchen.

8. Q: Who gave Erin some chocolates?
   A: Her teacher gave her some chocolates.

9. Q: Who helped the homeless?
   A: My grandfather helped the homeless.

10. Q: What made her upset?
   A: The weather made her upset.

11. Q: What was on the couch?
   A: My cat was on the couch.

PART 2

(A) 1. c 2. i 3. e 4. a 5. g
6. b 7. h 8. d 9. f

(B) 1. isn't he / Yes, he is.
2. aren't they / Yes, they are.
3. is he / No, he isn't.
4. do they / No, they don't.
5. isn't she / Yes, she is.
6. isn't it / Yes, it is.
7. isn't he / No, he isn't.
8. did she / Yes, she did.

UNIT 10 — Modal Verbs
조동사

PART 1

(A) 1. can't hear 2. couldn't pass
3. can't swim 4. can't find
5. couldn't watch 6. can't go
7. couldn't drive

(B) 1. Can / ride a bicycle / Yes, she can.
2. Can / ski well / No, he can't.
3. Can / fly an airplane / Yes, she can.

4. Can / open the jar / No, he can't.

5. Can / use a computer / Yes, she can.

PART 2

(A) 1. Can you be quiet, Tom?

2. Will you shut the door, please?

3. would you show me your notes?

4. Can you carry the box for me?

5. Will you answer my phone?

6. can you clean up your room?

7. Would you stop by on your way home?

8. Could you hold these files for a second, please?

PART 3

(A) 1. shouldn't drive   2. should work

3. should get   4. should talk

5. shouldn't watch   6. should apologize

7. shouldn't take   8. shouldn't blow

(B) 1. Should I buy this dress? / No, you shouldn't.

2. Should I invite Greg for dinner? / Yes, you should.

3. Should I go to class tomorrow? / Yes, you should.

4. Should I change tires? / Yes, you should.

5. Should I make a reservation? / Yes, you should.

6. Should I vote for Mr. Gordon? / No, you shouldn't.

7. Should I get a medical checkup? / Yes, you should.

(C) 1. don't have to   2. don't have to

3. has to   4. don't have to

5. Does / have to   6. Do / have to

(D) 1. Does he have to take the driving test again?

2. Do you have to exercise every day?

3. How much do I have to pay per each book?

4. How long does he have to stay in the training camp?

5. Do we / I have to work this Saturday?

6. Does Jane have to leave before 7?

(E) 1. have to   2. had to   3. has to

4. have to   5. have to   6. had to

(F) 1. mustn't   2. doesn't have to

3. mustn't   4. doesn't have to

5. mustn't   6. don't have to

PART 4

(A) 1. Would you like a cup of coffee? / Yes, please.

2. Would you like to play tennis? / No, thanks. I'm tired.

3. Would you like to go to the movies? / Yes, I'd love to.

4. Would you like to take a break? / Yes, I need to go to the restroom.

5. Would you like a sandwich? / No, thanks. I'm not hungry.

6. Would you like a piece of cake? / No, thanks. I'm on a diet.

7. Would you like to come to my birthday party? / Yes, thanks for inviting me.

8. Would you like to have dinner together? / No, I can't. I have plans.

(B) 1. Let's go clubbing.

2. Let's hurry.

3. Let's go home.

4. Let's take a class together.

5. Let's turn on the light.

6. Let's go to the supermarket.

7. Let's go to Bali.

8. Let's not drive.

Ⓒ 1. waiting → wait 2. eat not → not eat

3. going → go 4. joining → to join

5. not → don't 6. having → have

Ⓓ 1. **A:** Let's go clubbing tonight.

B: Sure, Let's go to Lucky Star.

A: Oh, I'm so excited.

2. **A:** I'm very exhausted. I'm out of energy.

B: Why don't we take a break?

A: Can we do that? We don't have much time to finish the project.

B: Well... I think we can. Why not take a short break?

A: OK. Let's continue after a short break.

3. **A:** Would you like to order?

B: Let's see... Hmm... Would you recommend something?

A: Of course. I recommend the lunch special. Today we have cream sauce pasta with shrimp.

B: Oh, that sounds good. I'd like to have that.

A: Sure. And would you like to order a drink?

B: I'll just have a glass of water, please.

A: Why don't you have a glass of soda? Soda is included in the lunch special.

B: Okay, then I will have Sprite.

UNIT 11 Simple Future Tense
미래시제

PART **1**

Ⓐ 1. won't 2. will 3. won't 4. won't

5. will 6. will, will

Ⓑ 1. I will study hard. / I won't skip the class.

2. I will drive more slowly. / I won't drive fast.

3. I will make you happy. / I'll take care of the kids together. / I'll share the housework.

4. I will keep the secret. / I won't tell anyone.

Ⓒ 1. She will call her friend in the morning / soon / later.

2. No, he won't.

3. He will go to the gym tonight.

4. They will stay at my house.

5. I will be back at 5:30.

6. Yes, they will.

7. Sam will give it to Danni.

8. They will take a bus.

9. Yes, he will.

Ⓓ 1. **A:** Andrew will quit his job.

B: That's sad. What will he do then?

A: I think he will look for a better job.

2. **A:** Hi, I have an appointment with Dr. Jones today at 3 o'clock.

B: I'm sorry, he's not here at the moment.

A: When will he be back?

B: I'm sure he will be back soon.

A: Then, I will be back in 5 minutes.

3. **A:** Wow! Did you hear the thunder?

B: Yes, I did. It's pouring. Will the rain stop soon?

A: Yes, it will. It's a rain shower. I'm sure it won't last long.

B: How do you know? Did you see the weather forecast?

A: Yes, I did. It will be sunny after the shower.

PART **2**

Ⓐ 1. b 2. c 3. g 4. a

5. d 6. e 7. f 8. h

B 1. So he <u>is going to fix</u> it.

2. So she <u>is going to take</u> a vacation.

3. They <u>are going to work out</u> at the gym tomorrow.

4. I <u>am going to ask</u> someone for help.

5. I <u>am not going to have</u> dessert.

6. I <u>am going to explain</u> it one more time.

7. The wedding ceremony <u>is going to begin</u> in a minute.

8. They <u>are not going to talk</u> to each other for a while.

C 1. They say it <u>is going to rain</u> tomorrow.

2. I <u>am going to spend</u> a week in Thailand.

3. He <u>is going to play</u> a lot of online games.

PART **3**

A 1. **Q:** Are you going to have lunch with us today?

2. **Q:** Are you / we going to move to a new place this weekend?

   A: No, we aren't. We are going to move next Tuesday.

3. **Q:** Is it going to snow tomorrow?

   A: No, it isn't. It's going to be sunny.

4. **Q:** Is he going to make a speech on Monday?

5. **Q:** Are you going to join a band?

   A: No, I'm not. I'm going to join a tennis club.

B 1. **Q:** Who are you going to meet this weekend?

   A: I'm going to meet Julia.

2. **Q:** Why are they going to sell their books?

   A: Because they have too many books.

3. **Q:** How are you going to get to the hospital?

   A: I am going to take a bus.

4. **Q:** When are we going to have dinner together?

   A: We're going to have dinner together next week.

5. **Q:** What is Jane going to tell you about?

   A: She is going to tell me about her plan.

C 1. **Chris:** What are you go(→ going) to do this weekend?

   Rachael: I am going to going(→ go) to the art gallery this Saturday.

   Chris: Wow! Who are you go(→ going to go) with?

   Rachael: With my roommate, Erin. Do you want to join us?

   Chris: I want to, but I watch(→ am going to watch) a movie with my girlfriend.

2. **Chad:** When(→ Where) are you going to move, Jasmine?

   Jasmine: Well... I'm going to moving(→ move) to a studio apartment next to the YMCA. Are you help(→ going to help) me move?

   Chad: Of course. Are(→ Is) Peter going to help you, too?

   Jasmine: No, he is(→ isn't). He's going (to) take the driving test on Friday.

   Chad: Then let's ask Ben for help as well.

PART **4**

A 1. is flying   2. are getting

3. is having   4. are going

5. Are, meeting   6. is, arriving, is arriving

7. are attending

B 1. **Q:** Are you coming to my wedding?

   A: Yes, I am.

2. **Q:** Is she going to work this weekend?

   A: No, she isn't.

3. **Q:** Are they playing baseball on Saturday?

   A: Yes, they are.

4. **Q:** Are you working on the weekends too?

   A: No, I'm not.

5. **Q:** Where are we going after lunch?

   A: We're going to a park.

6. **Q:** When are you leaving for your hometown?

   A: I'm leaving in March.

7. **Q:** Which airline are you taking to L.A.?

   A: I'm taking Singapore Airlines to L.A.

8. **Q:** What time is Harry arriving in Chicago?

   A: He's arriving at 6 pm.

Ⓒ 1. **Holly:** Are you working (P) on the report now?

   Adam: Yes, I am.

   Holly: You must be busy. Are you working (F) late today?

   Adam: Yes. I have to finish this report before my supervisor leaves for a business trip.

   Holly: When is he leaving (F)?

   Adam: Tomorrow morning.

2. **Steve:** Natalie, where are you going (P)?

   Natalie: Oh, I'm going (P) to the library now.

   Steve: I'm heading (P) that way, too. So, Natalie, what are you doing (F) after the final exam?

   Natalie: I'm staying (F) home because my parents are going (F) to visit me. How about you? What are your plans after the exam?

   Steve: I'm flying (F) to Thailand on June 25th.

   Natalie: Oh, really? When are you coming back (F)?

   Steve: In two weeks.

UNIT 12

Prepositions
전치사

PART 1

Ⓐ
in	2010	summer
	the afternoon	April
on	New Year's Day	June 6th
	weekends	December 11th, 1945
	Andy's birthday	Halloween
	Sam's day off	
at	quarter to twelve	Christmas
	noon	dinner
	the moment	midnight
	half past four	

Ⓑ 1. on   2. on   3. at   4. in

   5. at   6. In   7. on   8. at, on

Ⓒ 1. for   2. in   3. until   4. for

   5. during   6. in   7. until

Ⓓ **Steve:** What time do you usually wake up?

   Brooke: I usually wake up at 6 o' clock in the morning.

   Steve: Wow! Why do you get up that early?

   Brooke: Because I go to the gym on Monday, Wednesday, and Friday mornings.

   Steve: Why do you work out so much?

   Brooke: Because I have gained too much weight during the last year. I will lose 5kg in three months.

   Steve: Oh, wow! Good luck! Anyways, how long do you work out at a time?

   Brooke: I work out for an hour.

   Steve: So, when do you get to work?

   Brooke: I get to work at 9.

   Steve: I see. You are very diligent.

PART 2

Ⓐ 1. I parked my car <u>between</u> two dump trucks.

2. He dropped his key <u>under</u> the sofa.

3. I sat <u>near/in front of</u> the space heater because I was cold.

4. The bank is <u>next to</u> the supermarket.

5. The police car was right <u>behind</u> my car.

6. My family took a photo <u>in front of</u> the Statue of Liberty.

7. Tom always wants to sit <u>next to</u> Sally during meetings.

Ⓑ 1. on   2. at   3. on   4. at

5. at   6. at   7. at   8. in

Ⓒ 1. at   2. in   3. on   4. on, at

5. in   6. on   7. in   8. at

9. on, on   10. in

Ⓑ 1. e   2. b   3. f   4. d

5. a   6. c

Ⓒ 1. **Michael:** Laura, how do I download this picture?

   Laura: First, <u>move</u> the cursor to the picture. Then <u>click</u> the right mouse button and <u>press</u> 'save the picture'. <u>Type</u> in the name of the picture and then save it.

   Michael: Oh, now I get it.

2. **Jordan:** Excuse me, I'm a freshman here. How can I get to the auditorium?

   Kimberly: <u>Walk</u> straight up this street for one block and <u>turn</u> right. <u>Go</u> past the library and go through the tennis court. Then, you'll see the auditorium. You can't miss it.

   Jordan: Wow, this campus is huge. Thanks so much.

UNIT 13 — Imperatives
명령문

PART 1

Ⓐ 1. <u>Clean up</u> the room.   2. <u>Don't drive</u> too fast.

3. <u>Study</u> harder.   4. <u>Don't cry.</u>

5. <u>Get up.</u>   6. <u>Don't be late</u> for work.

7. <u>Wash</u> your car.   8. <u>Fasten</u> your seatbelt.

9. <u>Don't eat</u> food in the library.

10. <u>Watch</u> your step.

11. <u>Don't cheat</u> on the test.

PART 2

Ⓐ 1. Add   2. Pour   3. Chop   4. Bake

5. Mix   6. Stir   7. Grill   8. Microwave

UNIT 14 — Future Time Clauses
미래의 시간 부사절

PART 1

Ⓐ 1. If we (don't / won't) hurry, we (are going to be / are) late for class.

2. If it (will rain / rains / rain) tomorrow, I (won't go / don't go) hiking.

3. If we (stay / are staying) home tonight, we (watch / are going to watch) a movie.

4. We (play / will play) basketball if we (go / will go) to the park this Saturday.

5. People (will laugh / laugh) at you if you (go / are going) outside in that sweater.

6. I (wake / will wake) you up if I (got / get / will get) up early tomorrow.

7. If you (won't stop / don't stop) smoking, you

(will have / have / had) health problems.

8. You (will be / are) freezing if you (won't / don't) wear a coat.

(B) 1. If you dream of a pig, you will win a lottery.

2. If we take a day off tomorrow, we will go skiing.

3. If you buy your mother a gift, she will be pleased.

4. We will go swimming if the weather gets warmer.

5. If Mark makes more money, he will buy a new sports car.

6. I will be late for class if the bus comes late.

7. If Erica studies harder, she will pass the exam.

8. I will finish the project today if everyone helps me.

PART 2

(A) 1. When she has an interview, she will do great.
    1

2. He will come back to his office before his manager comes.
    2

3. After she gets a job, she will save money.
    1

4. I will help you when I have time next week.
    1

5. Before the summer vacation starts, I will lose weight.   2

6. When I go to Australia, I will definitely go to Bondi beach.   1

7. I will finish my report before the boss yells at me.
    2

8. He will take a bus after he gets off the subway.
    1

(B) 1. The salesperson will call you before she gets off from work.

2. When my friends visit my hometown, I will show them around.

3. After Eunice becomes a famous star, she will need a bodyguard.

4. While they are in Beijing, they will visit the Great Wall.

5. When he gets the job, he will celebrate it with his family.

6. Before I get married, I will travel around the world.

7. We will throw a surprise party when my dad comes home tonight.

8. Susan will go to bed right after she finishes her homework.

(C) 1. I will talk to you after I come back at 12.

2. While we are in Hong Kong, we will enjoy the night view.

3. Before he quits his job, he will look for a new job.

4. We will stay in a youth hostel when we get there.

5. While you are away, I will be busy with the term paper.

6. I will warm up before I go for a run.

7. When you are back from the business trip, I will buy you dinner.

UNIT 15 **Adjectives and Adverbs**
형용사와 부사

PART 1

(A) 1. Your dress is very pretty and unique.

2. Peter is my old friend.

3. She has brown eyes.

4. Susan has long black hair.

5. I didn't find anything strange in the room.

6. There isn't anything exciting here.

7. I need something unusual for the party.

8. There are many fancy restaurants in this town.

9. Rick bought an expensive car and a huge house.

10. The sushi in the restaurant is very fresh, and the prices are reasonable.

(B) 1. She is wearing a **long** dress.

2. Professor Dickinson gave me a **poor** grade.

3. This cup is **round and** big.

4. I love **spicy** Mexican food.

5. He has short **blond** hair.

6. All the people here are friendly **and clever**.

(C) 1. Sunday mornings are always peaceful and quiet.

2. We went to a big fancy restaurant.

3. Eunice has brown curly hair.

4. Look at this cute little baby.

5. I met a gentle Turkish man at the meeting.

6. I bought a black leather jacket yesterday.

7. I'd like to drink something cold and sweet.

8. I have a small cozy house.

PART 2

(A) 1. I like your wedding dress. You **look fabulous**.

2. Have you tried Indian food? It **tastes delicious**.

3. I like your idea. It **sounds brilliant**.

4. Are those roses? They **smell good**.

(B) 1. They look rich.

2. I don't feel tired.

3. He looks handsome.

4. The idea sounded clever.

5. It looks too big on you.

6. It tastes / smells really good.

7. She looks shocked.

8. Italian food looks / sounds / tastes / smells delicious.

PART 3

(A) 1. The news was very surprising to me.

2. Jody was confused by the directions.

3. I felt depressed after I saw the movie.

4. Julian had a tiring weekend.

5. The soccer match was very exciting.

6. I had a relaxing weekend.

7. Did you hear the shocking news today?

8. Christine is an interesting person.

(B) 1. The (shocking / shocked) news is on TV now.

2. Sorry for the (confusing / confused) information.

3. Everybody was happy with the (pleased / pleasing) news.

4. The (tired / tiring) people began to complain about the tour schedule.

5. The movie was so (touching / touched).

6. The show was very (surprising / surprised) to me.

7. Carrie is (interesting / interested) in science.

8. Mark and Pat felt so (boring / bored) at home.

(C) Dear Chris,

I have good news. Don't be surprised!!

I finally got a job at the *New York Times*!! Isn't this exciting? I'm so pleased. You know, I was so depressed when I didn't hear from any companies. I went through so many embarrassing moments in job interviews, and I was not sure about my future.

Anyway, I feel very relaxed now. Chris, I want to thank you for all your help.

Take care and see you soon.

Sincerely,

Jody

PART 4

(A)
1. They always (dress) badly.
2. Tim happily (waited) for the concert.
3. I (opened) the door slowly.
4. John and Simon (left) early.
5. Jenny (answered) correctly.
6. The dog (barked) loudly when the man entered the house.
7. Linda and Henry angrily (argued) over the matter.

(B)
1. He woke up early this morning.
2. I opened the box immediately.
3. Cathy plays the guitar excellently.
4. Christina looked back angrily.
5. Steven drives fast.
6. Dan goes to the gym regularly.
7. The children behave badly.
8. We decorated the Christmas tree beautifully.

(C)
1. Emily swims skillfully.
2. I learn things quickly.
3. The wind blows strongly.
4. Unfortunately, it began to rain.
5. It was very hot yesterday.
6. Gary speaks English well.
7. She danced beautifully at the contest.
8. James answered my questions honestly.

(D)
1. Mark is a fast runner.
2. Jon is a bad actor.
3. My father is a good cook.
4. Ella is a graceful dancer.
5. Susie is a hard worker.

(E)
1. Ron smokes heavily.
2. Ken works lazily.

3. Kelly talks quietly.
4. Dave plays soccer excellently.
5. Greg and Susan speak French fluently.

PART 5

(A)
1. I often visit my grandmother.
2. They always get to work on time.
3. He is never serious.
4. He rarely makes a mistake.
5. I sometimes read books before going to bed.
6. I am usually at the office in the morning.
7. We sometimes eat food late at night.
8. John never says bad things about other people.

(B)
1. Chris goes for a walk three times a week.
2. Chris does the laundry every Saturday.
3. Chris eats out every Friday.
4. Chris takes a day off once a month.
5. Chris goes shopping for clothes twice a month.

(C)
1. I brush my teeth every night.
2. I do the laundry once a week.
3. I often take a walk in the park with my sister in the morning.
4. I usually go to a bar at night.
5. Mary never works on the weekend.
6. Jake always checks his e-mails before midnight.
7. My family usually gets together twice a year.
8. I sometimes go to the library with my friend on Sunday.

UNIT 16 Comparatives and Superlatives
비교급과 최상급

PART 1

Ⓐ 1. softer
2. smarter
3. heavier
4. dirtier
5. smaller
6. more delicious
7. brighter
8. uglier
9. more handsome
10. newer
11. more slowly
12. later
13. more easily
14. earlier
15. better
16. faster
17. worse
18. less
19. more interesting
20. more fluently
21. harder
22. more
23. more quickly

Ⓑ 1. Helen speaks French <u>more fluently than</u> John.
2. The rabbit runs <u>faster than</u> the turtle.
3. Today, I feel <u>better than</u> yesterday.
4. Florida is <u>warmer than</u> Chicago.
5. Peter did <u>worse than</u> Robert on the math test.
6. The black car is <u>more expensive than</u> the white car.
7. Claire listens to the lecture <u>more carefully than</u> Andy.

Ⓒ 1. Mark is <u>taller than Don</u>.
2. Mark's hair is <u>shorter than Don's</u>.
3. Don is <u>heavier than Mark</u>.
4. Don is <u>older than Mark</u>.

PART 2

Ⓐ 1. hardest
2. earliest

3. youngest
4. most expensive
5. happiest
6. richest
7. most happily
8. most handsome
9. most useful
10. friendliest
11. hottest
12. loudest
13. laziest
14. most interesting
15. most slowly
16. biggest
17. most dangerous
18. shiniest
19. most fluently
20. best
21. worst
22. most
23. least

Ⓑ 1. the longest
2. the worst
3. the least carefully
4. the best
5. the most slowly
6. the hardest
7. the most expensive
8. the easiest
9. the most boring
10. the least interesting

Ⓒ 1. Alex <u>is the most delightful person</u>.
2. Edgar <u>is the laziest worker</u>.
3. Anna <u>is the funniest friend</u>.
4. Nicole <u>speaks the loudest</u>.
5. Megan <u>works the hardest</u>.
6. Rachel <u>is the most careful driver</u>.
7. Peter <u>spends the most money</u>.
8. Joseph <u>plays the piano the best</u>.

UNIT 17 Infinitives and Gerunds
부정사와 동명사

PART 1

Ⓐ 1. to write
2. to learn
3. to think
4. to visit
5. to study
6. to play

(B) 1. to buy   2. to see   3. to work

    4. to go to bed   5. to lose   6. me to have

    7. us to be   8. to make

(C) 1. He agreed <u>to</u> stay late.

    2. He told <u>me</u> to answer the phone.

    3. I hope <u>to</u> see you soon.

    4. I invited <u>him</u> to come over to my house this weekend.

    5. It is hard to <u>tell</u> the truth.

    6. It is always good to <u>see</u> you.

    7. It is always exciting <u>to</u> throw a party.

(D) 1. I <u>am afraid to drive</u> the car after the accident.

    2. I <u>am sad to hear</u> the news about your grandmother.

    3. I <u>was happy to see</u> all my friends at the party last week.

    4. She always <u>gets up</u> early <u>to go</u> to the gym.

    5. Everybody <u>studies</u> very hard <u>to pass</u> the exam.

    6. Yesterday, he <u>went</u> to the supermarket <u>to buy</u> some milk.

PART 2

(A) 1. smoking   2. to jog / jogging

    3. to spend / spending   4. to review

    5. sharing   6. to talk / talking

    7. asking   8. opening

(B) 1. talking   2. to play   3. to quit

    4. closing   5. to hold   6. writing

    7. watching   8. to give

(C) 1. baking   2. going   3. having

    4. taking   5. searching   6. hearing

PART 3

(A) 1. My boss let me go home early yesterday.

    2. I sometimes have my younger sister get milk on the way home.

    3. Ken always gets Cindy to set the alarm clock for 6 am.

    4. He had the waiter bring him a glass of water an hour ago.

    5. Professor Hanson let us hand in the final essay next week.

    6. Mr. Carrey got his assistant to finish the report this morning.

    7. The security guard didn't let us enter the building before 9:30 am.

    8. My boyfriend always makes me go home early.

(B) 1. Eric got Mindy <u>to</u> plan a ski trip this time.

    2. The boss made us <u>prepare</u> for the tomorrow's seminar.

    3. My physics teacher <u>let</u> us take a break for a moment.

    4. My housemate always makes me <u>cook</u> dinner.

    5. Yesterday, I had my assistant <u>make</u> a delivery for me.

    6. My mother doesn't let me <u>open</u> up the presents before Christmas.

    7. The parents had their children <u>only eat</u> homemade food.

    8. I got the housekeeper <u>to</u> clean up the room.

UNIT
18

Present Perfect Tense
현재완료 시제

PART 1

(A) 1. been   2. done   3. worked

4. visited   5. stopped   6. come
7. lived   8. forgotten   9. gone
10. had   11. made   12. seen
13. sung   14. spoken   15. spent
16. thought   17. played   18. eaten
19. tried   20. taken

Ⓑ 1. have never traveled   2. have lived
3. have had   4. Have you seen
5. Has he gone   6. have read
7. Have you eaten   8. has never smoked

Ⓒ 1. Ken hasn't played golf before.
2. I have lost my wallet twice.
3. Our team has won many games.
4. We have seen that movie three times.
5. Tom has studied Chinese before.
6. Mr. Smith has never tried Korean food.
7. I haven't visited New York before.

Ⓓ 1. I have never been to Italy.
2. I have seen the short film twice.
3. Have Susan and Rick ever been to Guam before?
4. My car has never broken down.
5. My sister has not been drunk before.
6. Has he won the championship?
7. I have taken the driving tests four times this year.

Ⓔ 1. Have you driven a convertible car before?
2. Have you watched the new movie?
3. Have you read *The Bible*?
4. Has James played the guitar before?
5. Have they taken a blood test?
6. Has she had any part-time jobs before?

PART 2

Ⓐ 1. since   2. for   3. since   4. for
5. since   6. for

Ⓑ 1. has been   2. have lived
3. has owned   4. has stayed
5. have known   6. have, had
7. has made

Ⓒ 1. Q: How long has James known Erica?
A: For a year.
2. Q: How long have you played the piano?
A: Since the age of five.
3. Q: How long has Ian been a police officer?
A: Since 2003.
4. Q: How long has she worked at a bank?
A: For two years.
5. Q: How long have you studied English?
A: Since last year.
6. Q: How long has Julie had the flu?
A: For a week.

UNIT
19   **Passives**
수동태

PART 1

Ⓐ 1. was cleaned   2. were sung
3. were painted   4. was written
5. was heard   6. were displayed
7. was held   8. was allowed

Ⓑ 1. The room wasn't cleaned a month ago.
2. The songs weren't sung by the singer in 2010.

3. The paintings weren't painted by Jackson Pollock.

4. The book wasn't written by Jane Austin in 1797.

5. Gary's voice wasn't heard from my office.

6. A lot of sculptures weren't displayed in the museum.

7. The conference wasn't held at the Johnson Company last week.

8. Parking wasn't allowed on Main St. last year.

(C) The Eiffel Tower

Have you heard of the Eiffel Tower? Do you know who designed it? The Eiffel Tower was designed by an engineer Gustave Eiffel and was completed in 1889. When it was built, it was named the world's tallest structure. However, when the Chrysler Building in New York City was constructed in 1930, the title was lost. Although it lost its title, it became the symbol of France. Now the Eiffel Tower is visited by millions of tourists every year.

(D) 1. were directed   2. are needed

3. was damaged   4. is picked up

5. were sent   6. is not spoken

7. were hurt

(E) 1. My car was stolen by a thief yesterday.

2. The baby was woken up by the noise.

3. The window was broken by the ball this morning.

4. Many old movies can be seen on TV.

5. The car wasn't fixed by the mechanic.

6. The ball point pen was invented by a Hungarian newspaper editor.

7. The decision was not made over the weekend.

8. The plants are not watered by Jack every day.

(F) 1. Q: Was lunch served at noon?

A: No, it wasn't. It was served at 1:00.

2. Q: Were the cars made in China?

A: Yes, they were.

3. Q: Was the schedule changed right before the meeting?

A: Yes, it was.

4. Q: Are the boxes delivered every day?

A: No, they aren't. They are delivered twice a week.

(G) 1. was, repaired   2. is, offered

3. were, canceled   4. was, written

UNIT 20

Relative Pronouns
관계대명사

PART 1

(A) 1. friend who lives in India

2. friend who loves rap music

3. people who work at the office

4. city that is famous for the Eiffel Tower

5. house which has big windows

6. woman who can speak four languages

7. books which are very difficult

(B) 1. that   2. who   3. who   4. which

5. who   6. which   7. who   8. that

(C) 1. I met a girl who lives in the suburbs.

2. There was a new book that has everything.

3. Andy is the man who is wearing a black jacket.

4. An orange is a kind of fruit that tastes a bit sour.

5. Teachers are the people who educate students.

6. This is the house that <u>is</u> close to the subway station.

7. A professional musician is a person who <u>plays</u> music for a living.

8. What's the name of the restaurant that <u>is</u> next to the drugstore?

(D) 1. I saw the old lady <u>who always wears a red muffler</u>.

2. Dane caught the boy <u>who broke the window</u>.

3. I am going to the grocery store <u>which/that opened yesterday</u>.

4. She fixed the car <u>which/that broke down</u>.

5. We met Dr. Tomlin <u>who is famous for his novels</u>.

6. This is the boy <u>who is from Australia</u>.

7. Dolphins are clever animals <u>which/that make people happy</u>.

8. Susie went to the movie theater <u>which/that was built 60 years ago</u>.

PART 2

(A) 1. ⟨hat⟩ that I got yesterday

2. ⟨apple⟩ that my mom bought yesterday

3. ⟨man⟩ who Julie is talking to

4. ⟨tomato soup⟩ that I made

5. ⟨book⟩ which I told you about yesterday

6. ⟨person⟩ who I talked about the other day

7. ⟨book⟩ that you're looking for

8. ⟨grandmother⟩ who I miss so much

(B) 1. Jenny is a student <u>who(m) everybody likes</u>.

2. There are some fashion magazines <u>which/that Jessica likes</u>.

3. My sister is holding a new bag <u>which/that I bought yesterday</u>.

4. Summer is the season <u>which/that I like the best</u>.

5. Where are the dogs <u>which/that I need to take care of for Linda</u>.

6. That's the toy <u>which/that my daughter likes to play with</u>.

7. She wore a mask <u>which/that she got for the costume party</u>.

8. This is my older brother <u>who(m) you met a month ago</u>.

(C) 1. that / object pronoun

2. that / subject pronoun

3. which / object pronoun

4. who / subject pronoun

5. who / subject pronoun

6. which / object pronoun

7. that / object pronoun

8. who / subject pronoun

(D) 1. The movie (that) I watched last night was fantastic. (✓)

2. The woman (who) we met at the party is going to get married soon. (✓)

3. Do you know the name of the Thai restaurant that is near the department store? (   )

4. The man (who) Sally is talking to is my roommate. (✓)

5. I bought a house which has four bedrooms. (   )

6. A violin is a musical instrument that has four strings. (   )

Listening Script

UNIT 01 Let's Speak!

Activity-1A

1. Robert
Hi, let me introduce myself. I am Robert. I am 28 years old, and I am single. I am an artist. I love my job. I am from England, but I am in Korea now. I am here to learn Korean culture. I am not really good at speaking Korean, but I am studying hard.

2. Danni
Hello, my name is Danielle, but you can call me Danni. I am 30 years old, and I am single. I'm from Canada, but I am in Thailand now. I am an English teacher. I like to teach students, so I am happy with my job. I want to teach English in Korea someday.

3. Ken
I'm Ken. I'm from America. I'm 35 years old. I'm married to a beautiful Korean wife. I have two lovely kids as well. I am a cook in a famous hotel, but the pay is not enough. So I want to change my job. I speak Korean well, so I think I can find a new job here in Korea.

Activity-2A

1. Thomas and Jane
My name is Thomas, and my wife is Jane. I'm from America, and my wife is from Thailand. We're having a great time in Korea now. We are here on business for three months. We're not good at speaking Korean, but our Korean friends help us with many things.

2. Tyler and Diana
Hi, I'm Diana and my friend's name is Tyler. We're from America. We are co-workers at an English language school here in Korea. Tyler is my only friend in Korea. He is nice and friendly. He helps me a lot with my everyday life. I am not good at speaking Korean, so I am going to study Korean.

3. Minho and Sarah
I want to tell you about my friends, Minho and Sarah. They are a lovely married couple. Minho is from Korea, and Sarah is from Canada. They speak good English and Korean. Minho and Sarah are in Canada now, so I miss them very much.

UNIT 02 Let's Speak!

Activity-2A

My name is Tom. There are five members in my family; my dad, my mom, older brother, younger sister and me. Oh, there is one more; my sister-in-law. My dad's name is Jason. He is a computer programmer. My mom's name is Lisa. She is a florist. She loves plants and flowers. My older brother's name is David. He is 33 years old. He is a car racer. He has his own sports car. He got married a year ago. His wife's name is Cathy. She is 29 years old. She is a writer. She writes children's books. David and Cathy have two puppies. So they take their puppies for a walk every morning. My younger sister's name is Wendy. She is 23 years old. She is an accessory designer. She makes many kinds of jewellery to sell. And I study photography. I want to become a professional photographer and have my own studio.

UNIT 03 — Let's Speak!

Activity-1A

1. My name is Nora. I come from Ottawa, Canada. I work at St. Peter's Hospital as a nurse. I like to drink my morning coffee at work. I drink coffee every morning. I don't like my busy schedule. I start work at 7 am and finish at 7 pm. I watch TV, cook, and sleep after work.

2. My best friend's name is Clare. She comes from America. She's a student. She studies accounting at the University of L.A. She likes to calculate numbers and sing. She doesn't like exams at school. She usually reads novels and relaxes after school.

3. Eric is my friend. He's from France and he is a journalist. He likes all sorts of digital cameras. He saves money to buy new cameras. He doesn't like traffic jams because it makes him late for work. He likes to exercise and have dinner with me after work.

Activity-2A

Ray: My name is Ray. I am a positive person. I don't get stressed easily. I go to the gym three times a week. I also try to eat breakfast every day.

Cathy: My name is Cathy. I get stressed easily. I sometimes get depressed and cry over small things. I don't exercise at all. And I don't usually eat breakfast because I usually get up at 10 o'clock.

Activity-3A

Q1: Where does James live?
A1: He lives in New York City.

Q2: What does he do?
A2: He is a web designer.

Q3: Where does he work?
A3: He works at an online game company.

Q4: What does he study every morning?
A4: He studies Chinese.

Q5: What do his co-workers think about him?
A5: They think he is nice and clever.

Q6: What does he usually do after work?
A6: He usually goes to the gym.

Q7: What does he do after he gets home?
A7: He watches his favorite shows online.

UNIT 04 — Let's Speak!

Activity-1B

1. You can write on the board using these. There are many different colors. What are they?

2. There are many of these in the classroom. Students sit on these. What are they?

3. This is hanging on the wall. This decorates the wall of the classroom. This is an artwork by a famous artist. What is it?

4. This is hanging on the wall. It is round. You can check the time. What is it?

UNIT 05 — Let's Speak!

Activity-3A

Hi, Emily. This is Daisy. What are you doing? Why are you not answering the phone? I'm just reading comic books at home. The sun is shining outside. I am just wondering about you. I hope you are not working. Call me back when you get my message. Talk to you soon.

Hey, Emily. This is Tim. I'm calling you from Bali. I'm spending my summer vacation here. This is a paradise. I'm enjoying my vacation a lot. People are swimming and drinking cocktails at the beach every day and night. Anyway, I'll call you again later. Bye.

Hi, Emily. This is Eunice. I'm at the new amusement park with Julia now. Thanks for recommending this place to us. We are having so much fun! Oh, the parade is beginning. Wow, this is so wonderful! Anyway, let's come here together next time.

UNIT 06 — Let's Speak!

Activity-3A

1. My name is Rosa. I was 24 when I started my first job as a kindergarten teacher. I was very nervous. Standing in front of little kids was really hard for me at first. But my co-workers helped me a lot. They were very nice to me. Also, the children were very sweet. It was a good experience.

2. My name is Aaron. I started my first job when I was 27. I worked for the marketing department at a company. I had to design many posters and brochures for the company. I was very excited about the work at first, but as time went by, the work became hard and stressful. My manager wasn't very nice either. Still, I believe it was a good experience for me.

3. I'm Tina. I was 18 when I had my first part-time job in a restaurant. I was a server. The work was hard for me in the beginning. I had to carry heavy dishes and serve the customers. Sometimes I broke dishes and took wrong orders from the customers. However, it was a good experience because I learned a lot about serving people.

UNIT 07 — Let's Speak!

Activity-1A

Last Saturday, I had a lot of work to do, so I went to the office. I canceled my tennis lesson because the work finished late. On Sunday, I had brunch at a restaurant with my college friends. Then, in the afternoon, I went to see a French movie with my boyfriend. I enjoyed it very much. When I got home, I went to bed early because I was tired. The next day, I got up late, so I didn't have breakfast.

UNIT 08 — Let's Speak!

Activity-3A

I was coming out of the bathroom yesterday when it happened. People were laughing at me while I was walking down the hallway. I didn't know why they were laughing. I found out the reason when I saw myself in the mirror. I was pulling along some toilet paper from the back of my pants! The toilet paper stretched all the way back to the bathroom.

UNIT 09 — Let's Speak!

Activity-2A

1. **A:** Ray didn't finish his final paper, did he?
   B: Yes, he did. He finished it already.

2. **A:** Today's presentation was very successful, wasn't it?
   B: Definitely, yes.

3. **A:** The manager canceled the meeting, didn't she?
   B: We are not sure yet.

4. **A:** That guy looks handsome, doesn't he?
   B: Hmm... I don't really agree with you.

5. **A:** Jade and Joy aren't twins, are they?
   B: Yes, they are.

6. **A:** I was just in time, wasn't I?
   B: Yes, you were.

UNIT 10 — Let's Speak!

Activity-4A

Conversation 1
A: Oh, I'm starving.
B: Would you like a piece of cake? I have some in my refrigerator.
A: Sure! Why not?

Conversation 2
A: We have so much work. I'm so exhausted.
B: Why don't we hire more workers?
A: Unfortunately, we can't. We don't have money for that.

Conversation 3
A: The summer holidays are coming up soon.
B: Yay! I'm really looking forward to the summer holidays.
A: Me, too. Let's go rafting together.
B: Oh, I'm afraid I can't go rafting. I am scared of water.

Conversation 4
A: I spend a lot of time thinking about what to wear to work every morning.
B: Me, too. I need more winter clothes.
A: Then, would you like to go shopping this Saturday?
B: I've already got plans this Saturday. What about Sunday?
A: I'll be out of town on Sunday. Let's go another day then.

UNIT 11 — Let's Speak!

Activity-3A

My name is Julie. I am a senior at a university now. I am going to graduate next year. My family and all my friends will be so proud of me. We will take a lot of photos.

My name is Brian. I am going to quit my job early next year. I am working on my résumé and doing some research into new jobs these days. I will find a new job soon.

My name is Lily. I am pregnant. I'm expecting a baby in June of next year. So my husband and I are going to be parents soon. I am looking forward to being a mom.

I'm Vincent. Next year, I'm going to take some time off from school and study abroad. I'd like to study English. So I'm going to take a language course in Australia. There, I'll try to make many Australian friends and learn a lot about their culture.

I'm Elaine. I'm going to go backpacking around Western Europe next year. I'm going to France, Switzerland, and Italy. I'm learning French these days. I hope I can talk to French people while visiting France.

I'm Minho. I'm 21 years old. I'm going to join the army next year. I'm going to be in the army for two and a half years. I will miss my parents and my girlfriend.

UNIT 12 — Let's Speak!

Activity-1A

December is just around the corner. I'm very excited that I have lots of special plans.
On December 9th, I am going to meet Mina at 1 pm

at Mega Mall. On the same day, Mina and I are going to see a Jazz concert at 5 pm.

My dad's birthday is on December 11th. We are going to have a party at the Grand Restaurant at 6 pm.

Then, on the third Saturday, my cousin, Susie, is getting married. So, I am going to go to the hair salon that morning.

I am going to meet my boyfriend on Christmas Eve and watch a movie. Also, I'm going to church at 10 pm that night.

On Christmas day, I'll have a family gathering until 5 pm and go clubbing with my friends at 6 pm.

My winter holiday is from December 29th to January 3rd. So, during the holiday, I am going on a trip to Japan.

 Let's Speak!

Activity-2

Welcome to the *Everybody Can Cook Show*. Today, we are going to make tomato sauce spaghetti. It's really easy and quick to make! First, boil some water. Then, put spaghetti in the boiling water and boil it for about 8 to 10 minutes. While the spaghetti is boiling, chop some onions and garlic. Then, put the tomato sauce in the pan and add the chopped onions and garlic to the sauce. Cook the sauce over medium heat. Then, place the spaghetti on the plate. Pour the tomato sauce on the spaghetti and enjoy!

Activity-3A

1. **A:** How do I get to the high school?
   B: Go straight for two blocks and turn right at Queen's Street. Then you'll see it on your left.

2. **A:** How do I get to the church?
   B: Go straight for one block and turn left. Walk past the bank. You'll see it on your left.

3. **A:** How do I get to the flower shop?
   B: Go straight on King's Street and turn right on City Hall Street. Go straight and you'll see it on your left, next to the post office.

4. **A:** Where is the fountain?
   B: Go straight for two blocks and turn left at Queen's Street. Go straight past Church Street. Then you'll see it on your right.

5. **A:** How can I get to the coffee shop?
   B: Go straight on King's Street to Queen's Street. Then turn left. It's on your right next to the snack bar.

 Let's Speak!

Activity-1A

Conversation 1

Jason: Erica, what will you do if you take a day off?

Erica: Well... If I take a day off, I will go to the hospital for a medical check-up.

Jason: Oh! That's a very good idea.

Erica: What about you, Jason? What will you do if you take a day off?

Jason: I'll sleep all day long.

Conversation 2

Adam: Hana, what will you do if you become a manager?

Hana: Well... If I become a manager, I will lead the team with a sincere heart. What about you, Adam?

Adam: Hmm... I will be a strict manager if I become a manager. I will punish my team members if they are late for work.

Hana: Oh, no.

Conversation 3

Sean: Hailey, do you have a boyfriend?

Hailey: Yes, I do. Why?

Sean: Hmm... What will you do if your boyfriend cheats on you?

Hailey: I will break up with him. What will you do if your girlfriend cheats on you, Sean?

Sean: I will track down the guy and punch him in his face.

Hailey: Ooh. Calm down.

UNIT 15 · Let's Speak!

Activity-1A

1. a. The woman is slim.
   b. Her hair is in a ponytail.
   c. She is wearing a long track suit.

2. a. A young Korean couple is getting married.
   b. They are wearing a traditional Korean attire called *Han-bok*.
   c. They look very tired.

3. a. He is chubby.
   b. He is wearing a black hat.
   c. He is wearing round glasses.

4. a. The girl is wearing a dress.
   b. She is carrying a tiny little bag.
   c. She has curly hair.

Activity-3A

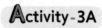

Conversation 1
A: How was your weekend?
B: I spent the whole weekend by myself. I felt time went by so slowly during the weekend.

Conversation 2
A: Why is your face so red?
B: I slipped and fell in the street. There were lots of people behind me. I wanted to hide somewhere.

Conversation 3
A: Are you satisfied with your final exam grade?
B: Satisfied? Are you joking? I can't believe Professor Anderson gave me an F on my final.

Conversation 4
A: I gave a presentation yesterday.
B: Oh, how did it go?
A: I felt my legs shaking during my talk. My voice was shaking, too.

UNIT 16 · Let's Speak!

Activity-1A

1. My name is Rebecca. Recently, two men proposed to me. Ryan is one year older than me. He likes all kinds of sports and likes to cook for me. He is the funniest and sweetest person I know. But he doesn't make a lot of money. On the other hand, Derrick owns his own business and makes a lot of money. He is seven years older than me. Derrick buys me many things, but we have nothing in common. Also, it's boring to be with him because he always talks about his business.

2. I'm Kelly. I have two younger brothers. John is 16 years old, and Chris is 12 years old. John likes candy and biscuits, so he eats them all the time. However, Chris doesn't like sweets. That's why John weighs 78kg and Chris only weighs 55kg. John has many friends at school, so he often brings his friends home. On the other hand, Chris is quiet at school. He doesn't talk much or play a lot. Chris always studies both at school and at home. He is the top student in his ·class.

3. My name is Chris. I am the manager of a publishing department. I have to recommend one of my workers for Employee of the Year. I have two people in mind. One is David and the other is Linda. David is 6 years older than Linda. He works extra hours during weekends and works faster than Linda. However, he often gets to work late and argues with me a lot. Linda works harder than David during regular working hours, but she works slower than David. She gets to work early and gets along well with me.

UNIT 17 Let's Speak!

Activity-4A

Conversation 1

Julie: Tim, could you make 30 copies of this?

Tim: Sure. I'll photocopy them right after I finish typing this document.

Julie: Thanks. I just need them before the meeting.

Tim: OK. They will be ready by then.

Conversation 2

Peter: Did you check the notice board in front of Professor Rhee's office?

Julie: No, I didn't. What did it say?

Peter: We must hand in our report before this month is over.

Julie: I thought it was due next month. Why did he change the deadline?

Peter: Because he's going to a seminar in Russia next month.

Conversation 3

Ron: Ms. Kelly, can I take a week off next month?

Ms. Kelly: A whole week off?

Ron: Yes. Is that OK?

Ms. Kelly: Hmm... I'm afraid we have a lot to do next month.

Conversation 4

Mom: Tom, we're out of milk and cereal. Can you go get some groceries after lunch?

Tom: I'd like to help you, mom, but I have to go to the marathon practice.

Mom: It won't take that long. I'm really busy with other things.

Tom: OK, then. I'll do it.

UNIT 18 Let's Speak!

Activity-1A

Conversation 1

W: Have you ever traveled abroad?

M: Yes, I've been to Europe, America and Canada before. How about you?

W: Hmm... I've never traveled to other countries before. But, I've been to Jeju Island many times.

M: I haven't been there. I want to go there someday.

Conversation 2

W: Have you used the Internet recently?

M: Yes, I have. Why?

W: Have you found anything strange?

M: No, I haven't. What's wrong?

W: I think the Internet connection hasn't worked well recently.

M: Really? Mine works fine.

Conversation 3

M: Your English pronunciation is good. Have you lived in an English speaking country before?

W: Yes. I've lived in Singapore.

M: How long have you lived there?

W: I've lived there for three years.

M: I see. I've never lived in another country.

UNIT 19 Let's Speak!

Activity-2A

Ladies and gentlemen, this is the captain speaking. Our plane will be landing shortly at Heathrow Airport, London. So please make sure your seatbelts are tightly fastened and your cellphones are turned off. Make sure that all the items in the overhead bins are safely stowed, and all your carry-on bags are placed under your seats. Thank you very much and I hope you enjoyed the flight.

UNIT 20 Let's Speak!

Activity-2A

She is a very famous TV talk show host. She lives in the United States. She was the first woman to anchor a major newscast in the U.S. She started her own production company NELLA. NELLA is named after her mother. She has produced several TV shows. They became very popular.